Fitness, Racquet Sports, and Spa Projects

FITNESS, RACQUET SPORTS, AND SPA PROJECTS:

A Guide to Appraisal, Market Analysis, Development, and Financing

Arthur E. Gimmy, MAI and Brian B. Woodworth

  American Institute of Real Estate Appraisers
430 North Michigan Avenue
Chicago, Illinois 60611-4088

For Educational Purposes Only

The opinions and statements set forth herein do not necessarily reflect the viewpoint of the American Institute of Real Estate Appraisers or its individual members, and neither the Institute nor its editors and staff assume responsibility for such expressions of opinion or statements.

Printed in the United States of America
92   91   90   89   5   4   3   2   1

Library of Congress Cataloging in Publication Data

Gimmy, Arthur E.
    Fitness, racquet sports, and spa projects : a guide to appraisal, market analysis, development, and financing / prepared by Arthur E. Gimmy and Brian B. Woodworth.
      p.   cm.
    Bibliography: p.
    ISBN 0-911780-98-X : $21.00
    1. Leisure industry. 2. Physical fitness centers—Economic aspects. 3. Marketing. I. Woodworth, Brian B. II. Title.
GV188.G55   1989
338.4'7790'013—dc19
                                88-31518
                                     CIP

Table of Contents

List of Tables, Charts and Figures

Foreword

This monograph is an updated and expanded version of the appraisal manual on racquet sports facilities that the Appraisal Institute published in 1978. Over the years racquet sports have diminished in popularity while a variety of other physical activities have gained more prominence. The focus of this book, therefore, extends beyond racquet sports projects to encompass diverse, urbanized recreational facilities that are being developed to meet continuously evolving recreational activities.

The purpose of this monograph is to discuss the facets that must be considered in evaluating a fitness/recreational facility. The book presents the basic trends and characteristics of the recreational industry and provides guidelines for determining the feasibility of a project and estimating its value.

The Appraisal Institute gratefully acknowledges the contributions of Arthur E. Gimmy, MAI, who wrote the original monograph, and Brian B. Woodworth, who collaborated with Mr. Gimmy in preparing this updated and expanded version. The Appraisal Institute also wishes to express its thanks to Richard Marchitelli, MAI, Chairman of Publications; John J. Healy, Jr., MAI; James H. Bulthuis, MAI; David J. Lau, MAI; and John A. Schwartz, MAI, who acted as reviewers of the monograph.

J. Carl Schultz, Jr., MAI
1989 President
American Institute of
Real Estate Appraisers

Preface

Recreational projects can be highly profitable, and this factor is a driving force behind market supply and growth patterns. The industry, however, is also characterized by rapid changes in demand; while these forces create continual need for professional evaluations, it also compounds the difficulties facing the appraiser in the analysis of existing and proposed recreational developments. Difficulties in valuation are further aggravated by the actual nature of the business. Operating, rental, and sales data, for example, are often difficult to obtain and inconsistent in presentation.

The preparation of this research project was particularly challenging due to the industry's constant state of flux and the diverse and multifaceted projects that compose the market. We wish to thank the International Racquet Sports Association (IRSA) for the use of their materials in this book. IRSA's research and publications are an excellent source of information for this industry. Their annual reports should be consulted for the updated industry operating statistics.

The book is designed as a reference source for the appraiser, developer, builder, lender, owner, and manager involved with fitness and recreational projects. Detailed information on design, construction materials, lighting, heating and ventilation, equipment, and furnishings is not presented because such information is available from industry magazines and specialized publications. Specific construction costs also are not emphasized in this book because they vary considerably by region and change significantly over time.

Acknowledgments

The authors are grateful to Carla Matlin for her assistance with this project. Her research, writing, and organizational abilities contributed greatly to the quality of this book. Carla's achievements are especially noteworthy considering the complex challenge the nature of this industry presents and the time she sacrificed from her MBA program at the University of California, Berkeley. We wish her well in her career.

We also wish to thank the word processing staff of the Arthur Gimmy International for their contribution to this effort. Additional thanks and credit are given to the Publications Committee of the American Institute of Real Estate Appraisers.

About the Authors

Arthur E. Gimmy, MAI, is President and owner of Arthur Gimmy
International, a real estate appraisal and consulting firm based in San
Francisco, California. Since 1955, Mr. Gimmy has had extensive
experience in valuation counseling and expert testimony on all types of
properties on a nationwide basis. Mr. Gimmy holds a Bachelor of Science
in Business Education and a Master of Education from the University of
California at Los Angeles. In addition to membership in the Appraisal
Institute, he is a member and past-president of Valuation Network, Inc., a
nationwide consortium of leading appraisal firms throughout the United
States. Mr. Gimmy has contributed to the *Appraisal Journal* and other
business publications. He is the author of two books published by the
Appraisal Institute: *Tennis Clubs and Racquet Sports Projects* (1978) and
Elderly Housing (1988). In addition to appraisals of fitness, racquet
sports and spa facilities, Mr. Gimmy has appraised a variety of
recreational properties, including PGA-rated golf courses, tropical resorts
and full-scale country clubs.

Brian B. Woodworth is an appraisal associate with Arthur Gimmy
International and directs their Lodging/Recreational Properties Division.
Since 1985, Mr. Woodworth has appraised and conducted market
analyses of a variety of commercial and special purpose property types.
Mr. Woodworth holds a Bachelor of Arts in Political Science and
Economics from Boston University and a Master of City and Regional
Planning from Harvard University. Mr. Woodworth has engaged in
extensive research regarding the recreational industry since 1987.

Introduction

America at Play

Move over, "Sedentary Sam," the age of armchair athletics has given way to physical participation. Americans are seeking recreational activities in more numerous and active forms than ever before.

A.C. Nielsen Company, a prominent market research firm, tracked sports activity from 1973 through 1982. Their survey data reveal an increasing and stable trend in American sports participation.

Table 1.1 American Sports Participation

Year	Number of Participants	Percentage of Change
1973	205,950,000	
1976	210,019,000	+2%
1979	214,958,000	+2%
1982	225,598,000	+5%

Source: A.C. Nielsen Company.

A comparison of the statistics from the 1965 and 1982 National Recreational Surveys, conducted by the Census Bureau for the Department of the Interior, also indicates a shift toward more active participation. The proportion of Americans who participated in passive recreational activities—picnicking, pleasure driving, and sightseeing—declined while the proportion of Americans partaking in active pursuits, such as tennis, weight training, bicycling, skiing, hiking, and canoeing, increased.

More recent statistics are provided by the Gallup Opinion Index, which has annually polled selected sports activities since 1959. In 1961 24% of American adults exercised on a regular basis. By 1980 this number jumped to 46%, and in 1986 a 51% majority claimed participation in some type of fitness program. Table 1.2 highlights the trends for selected activities. It can be seen from the table that swimming and bicycling continue to be America's favorite sport activities. Jogging, tennis, and racquetball, which have fallen from the media's graces as "trendy chic," nevertheless still maintain strong participatory rates.

Table 1.2 Gallup Opinion Index Percent Participation

Activity	1986	1985	1984	1980	1972	1966
Swimming	43%	41%	41%	37%	42%	33%
Jogging	28	23	18	12		
Weight Training	21	19				
Aerobics, Dancercise		18				
Golf	12	13	12	8	14	11
Bowling	22	25	21	24	28	27
Softball	22	22	18	16	13	15
Camping	25	21		19		
Tennis	12	13	11	14	12	9
Racquetball	5-9	8		6		
Calisthenics	20	15				
Volleyball	20	16	14	13	12	12
Basketball	19	15		18		
Hiking	25	18		21		
Bicycling	35	33		27		

Findings are based on in-person interviews with a national sample of adults who were shown a list of more than 50 sports and recreational activities and were asked to name those in which they had participated within the previous 12 months.

Source: Gallup Opinion Polls, *Gallup Leisure Activities Index 1986* (Princeton: 1986), p. 9.

Why We Play

The fitness industry, as a whole, has seen an exercise explosion over the past ten years. But why? What accounts for this increased participation in physical activities? There are many motivating factors, and almost all of them underscore the importance people attach to fitness as contributing to their quality of life.

The "body beautiful" has probably been the number one motivator for a variety of people. Almost everyone is concerned about personal appearance, and many people choose to exercise to shape up, slim down, or simply maintain their weight and body tone. For many others, an exercise regime is prescribed therapy for heart disease, hypertension, diabetes, and other health concerns.

In both these cases people are choosing exercise to attain an end goal. But exercise is not necessarily all work and no enjoyment. Many people participate in physical activities "just for the fun of it." As Americans grow more affluent and have greater flexibility in their work hours, they look to increase and broaden their leisure time activities. Participation in sports and recreational pursuits adds excitement and thrills to everyday living. It satisfies drives for competition and releases energy, which leads to sensations of exhilaration and vitality.

The concept of exercise has changed dramatically since the mid-1960s when the term exercise conjured up images of laborious drudgery in dismal gymnasiums. Now it is "cool" to sweat. Being athletic is a status symbol, and those who are not truly athletic can at least look the part by wearing sport clothes and "making the scene" at the local health club. Sport activities offer opportunities for social interaction, and health clubs have capitalized on that notion. The health club juice bars have become the singles bars of the 1980s.

Yet no matter what the motivating factor is, medical researchers concur that what is good for the body is also good for the mind; physical fitness improves mental fitness. The physical exertion of exercise instills feelings of accomplishment and reward; it feeds the ego and lifts the spirits. In addition to pepping up the psyche, exercise improves mental fitness by helping people cope with stress. Keeping pace with today's lifestyle often takes its toll in the form of anxiety and muscular tension, conditions that precipitate the onset of more serious health complications. Exercise offers a release of this tension and a way to relax that is more effective, healthier and less expensive than the use of drugs or medical treatments.

In recent years these benefits of physical exercise on mental and physical health have been related to work performance. Studies revealed that an employee exercise program promotes a more effective work experience for the employee. Participants in these studies reported greater stamina, increased energy, and a more positive work attitude following an exercise workout. For instance, a Texas-based Fortune 500 company found in 1984 that workers who exercise regularly average 27 hours of sick leave and $173 in health costs per year, compared to 44 hours and $434 for inactive workers.[1]

Corporate America is beginning to recognize the validity of these findings. Company after company has either opened their own fitness center or has arranged special reduced-cost corporate memberships for employees at private health clubs. A recently completed study by the federal Department of Health & Human Services found that 60% of the 1,358 worksites surveyed had some type of health promotional activity.[2]

How We Play

Americans are hard at play, but how do they play and where do they play? The answer reads like a veritable social register. Nearly all categories of active sport and recreational activities are reporting growth statistics; and, referring again to the Gallup Poll Index in Table 1.2, those activities that rode the boom and bust wave of faddishness have now settled into more of a continuum. Their numbers are still strong and stable. Tennis, for example, peaked in 1980 with 14% participation but fell to 11% in 1984; today it is climbing back up and has a 12% to 13% participation rate.

According to the National Sporting Goods Association, sporting goods sales were well above $15 billion in 1984, and by 1986 the sales figures had jumped more than 80% to $27.5 billion.[3] Home exercise equipment sales alone topped $960 million in 1984. This figure is more than twice the sales in 1982.[4] Analysts explain the surge in home fitness as being economically motivated. Many people who once regarded home equipment as too expensive now find that a good machine costs less than a health club membership.

Industrywide growth rates for commercial fitness centers (defined in this instance as centers using weight equipment like that made by Universal and Nautilus) can be estimated by the expansion of health club chains. In 1970 the Health and Tennis Corporation, owned by Bally Manufacturing Corporation, had 57 fitness clubs. In 1985 this chain included 323 clubs. In 1980 the clubs had a total membership of about 1 million. By 1984 that number had grown to 1.6 million, generating $335 million in revenue and $85 million in gross profit.[5]

The waves of recreational demand open the door to innumerable development alternatives. Real estate developers have been quick to discern the implications recreational trends hold for business. One of the newest implications is that athletic clubs can help sell and lease office space. A Richmond, Virginia, office development was recently constructed with a 3,000 square foot exercise facility, complete with locker rooms and sauna. The building's tenants consider the fitness facility an amenity; the developer considers it a marketing tool.[6]

Historical Overview

The period leading up to the 1970s was marked by an affluent burgeoning middle and upper-middle class that was, because of the post-World War II baby boom, very family-oriented. Suburbia was born, and new types of commercial recreational projects appeared.

The YMCAs/YWCAs are the oldest formally established health and physical fitness centers in the United States. They opened their doors as early as the 1860s. However, these nonprofit establishments were not developed solely as fitness centers. Rather, their original charters are committed to providing a variety of community services—vocational and cultural as well as recreational—to all audience segments.

Following the success the early Ys experienced, other denominations formed equivalent organizations; most notable are the Jewish Community Centers (JCCs), which are located in nearly all major metropolitan areas. Today YMCAs/YWCAs and JCCs still hold to their community service commitments, but their health and fitness amenities are rivaling private counterparts.

Like the Y, private country clubs responded to a need for family-oriented sports, team activities, and recreational opportunities. But whereas the Y has a no-frills community approach to physical fitness that is built around swimming and gymnasium programs, the country club emphasizes an air of luxury and exclusiveness that is built around the golf course.

The 1950s and 1960s saw the advent of today's modern health club. In the 1960s, however, the operations termed themselves *health spas* (today's definition of a health spa is much different and will be discussed in Chapter 2), and their emphasis was on relaxation amenities such as whirlpools, steam rooms, saunas, and massage. Pools were small and were built for dipping rather than swimming laps; exercise equipment was minimal, consisting of standard resistance machines for male members and passive nonstrenuous equipment for female members.

In contrast, the 1970s and 1980s witnessed a proliferation in types of athletic clubs, court clubs, and fitness studios. At one end of today's spectrum are operations designed solely for an exercise workout. For example, a Los Angeles-based chain offers coin-operated racquetball courts with no locker room or shower; it is strictly a court with coin-operated admittance. The other end of the spectrum is dedicated to personal pampering. These are the health/fitness spas of the 1980s whose facilities surround guests with sumptuous luxury and elegance.

Between these extremes are the more typical health and physical fitness clubs. These are the facilities that appeal to mainstream America and satisfy needs for recreation, body toning, weight control, health restoration, physical and mental wellness, and social interaction.

Contents

This book discusses the health and physical fitness industry both in terms of the types of facilities that are predominant in the market and in terms of political, legal, and business issues confronting the industry. Its specific purpose is to assist the reader in the analysis of existing or proposed fitness facilities. It examines the factors relevant to understanding and implementing a market study, a financial evaluation, a business assessment, and a real estate appraisal.

Chapter 1 introduces the historic patterns, trends, and motivating factors that are having impact on developer interest in the health and fitness industry. Chapter 2 describes the gamut of recreational facilities covered in this book. In addition to facility types, this chapter outlines design factors and construction trends that currently are shaping the industry.

In Chapter 3 site considerations are discussed with particular attention paid to land costs, location, size, zoning, and competition. Competitiveness in the fitness industry has become fierce and includes controversial profit versus nonprofit status issues. Chapter 4 describes demographic characteristics and trends that influence market demand. Factors that influence market feasibility analyses are derived from this background information.

With Chapter 5 the book turns to the operating side of the fitness industry. This chapter focuses on how management functions. Profitability in the fitness industry requires much more than a well-designed, well-targeted facility. Management is a key factor that is often overlooked. In addition, Chapter 5 covers the ongoing debate concerning government and industry regulation. These issues will have major ramifications for future trends in the industry.

Many fitness facilities throughout the United States have filed for bankruptcy in recent years. Chapter 6 addresses the financing issues that concern lenders when evaluating loan applications from health and fitness developers. This chapter presents and analyzes the results of an extensive survey of major lenders throughout the United States, which questioned their views of the fitness industry.

Chapter 7 offers a "how-to" approach to determining a facility's economic feasibility. The important components stressed in this discussion include target market identification, site review and competitive analysis, market demand quantification, operating forecasts, and return on investment analysis.

The actual appraisal process is examined in Chapter 8. Factors influencing the process, approaches to valuation, and any special considerations that may arise are discussed from an appraiser's perspective.

Chapter 9 presents detailed case studies including project and valuation statistics. The studies provide operating revenue and expense data for several types of facilities to give a general picture of variations in the industry. This chapter illustrates real world problems of analyzing commercial recreational facilities.

Finally, in Chapter 10 we summarize the findings from our research. Conclusions are presented on the current state of the fitness industry, and we offer our predictions for the future of the industry in terms of development, feasibility, and valuation.

Types of Recreational Facilities

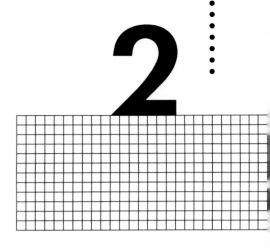

More fitness clubs and other types of clubs are in business today than ever before. During the past ten years, as the fitness industry exploded, specialization and niche marketing became the reigning operational schemes. The strategy was that the facility dedicated to a single activity would operate in the most efficient and cost-effective manner. As time progressed, however, the strictly single-sport club has faded in prominence and, in general, in profitability.

Consumer tastes have bounded from one activity to another, and facilities have quickly restructured to keep in step with the movement. Tennis clubs added weight training areas. Racquetball clubs made room for aerobic studios. In all, the boundaries that once defined and distinguished racquet clubs from weight training centers have become soft and ambiguous. An enlightened, health conscious America quickly attached the label *health club* to a vast array of facility types. Given such diversity in facilities, this chapter will define the health club industry in terms of six categories:

- *Tennis Clubs*. Several variations on the classic tennis club have emerged. In addition to the traditional outdoor club, there are "hardtop" clubs, indoor-outdoor combinations, a growing number of tennis resorts, and residential projects with tennis facilities.

- *Court Clubs.* Racquetball, handball, and squash players require specialized facilities. Once, these facilities were dedicated solely to racquet activities; now the clubs are adding more options to retain old members and attract new ones.

- *Multisport Athletic Clubs.* The label *health club* is most appropriately used in reference to these multifaceted facilities. The clubs offer full-service sports and fitness opportunities to the consumer on a scale that ranges from the basic YMCA to the luxurious urban country club.

- *Storefront Operations.* Weight training centers and aerobic studios fall under this category. In sheer numbers alone, these types of facilities dominate the fitness industry; and, because of their relatively small space requirements, they can be found in a variety of locales: in malls, in office buildings, and above, below, or inside street-level shops.

- *Profit Centers.* Some consider fitness a national obsession. To capitalize on that opportunity, fitness facilities are being constructed as add-on amenities and profit centers in hotels, airports, hospitals, and apartment complexes.

- *Health Spas.* The fitness vacation is the newest trend. Visitors can choose a vacation spa that emphasizes rest, recreation, and personal pampering, or the spa can be more focused—for example, to provide weight loss or health rejuvenation programs. Expanding on this concept is an emerging club type known as "spa clubs." The spa club targets a permanent population with a vacation spa focus.

Each of the above mentioned facility types is described below on a much more detailed basis. Included is a discussion of the physical characteristics of each facility type, with information highlighting unique layout, design, and construction issues.

Tennis Clubs

The appraiser faced with a tennis project will generally be concerned with one of five types of tennis facilities: the traditional outdoor tennis club, the indoor tennis club, the indoor/outdoor combination tennis club, the tennis resort, or the residential project with tennis facilities. Although all facilities share certain common aspects, each has its unique marketing and construction problems that require separate treatment.

Suburban-type outdoor clubs have existed for many years. Before the racquetball surge, these tennis clubs were the dominant type of court facility found in the United States. Climate conditions, however, set limits to the development opportunities for outdoor clubs. The majority of newer clubs are being built in the West and Southwest, where tennis usually can be played outdoors up to 320 days per year.

Ten years ago the typical outdoor club had six to ten tennis courts, an outdoor swimming pool, a clubhouse, small pro shop, snack bar, and locker room. Today, tennis clubs are adding complementary amenities. Weight machines and cardiovascular equipment are often standard features. The social element is enhanced with limited-menu restaurants replacing the snack bars.

The advent of the indoor tennis club increased tennis participation across the country, but most particularly in the Northeast and Midwest where outdoor tennis playing was limited to five months a year.

Indoor clubs are normally housed in warehouse-like prefabricated steel structures, in converted concrete tilt-up and wood-frame buildings, or in air-pressure supported plastic bubbles. They generally hold 4 to 12 tennis courts, a reception area, locker rooms, pro shop, and snack area. More elaborate clubs will also offer exercise rooms, facilities for other racquet sports, indoor swimming pools, saunas, steam rooms, and whirlpools.

The cost of construction is a critical factor to the economics of the club, and expensive structures can rarely be justified. The metal or prefabricated building is most popular because it is a permanent structure that is easily erected at a relatively reasonable price. There are many manufacturers in the field, and competition has resulted in an emphasis on attractive design and overall appearance. Such structures also have the advantage of convertibility to warehouses or light industrial uses and are easily insulated for use in a variety of climates. This type of design can interface with a clubhouse of a different construction material, such as a combination of concrete block and native stone, that can result in a country club appearance. The main disadvantage of metal buildings, other than cost, is that they are permanent and do not offer facilities for players who may want to play outside at certain times of the year.

An alternative to the prefabricated building is the air-supported and tension structure known as a *bubble*. It is manufactured from high-strength, vinyl-coated polyester material and is equipped with stress relief systems and a thermal liner. It can be used to cover existing tennis courts, providing weather protection at a relatively low initial cost. One that is large enough to cover four tennis courts currently is priced at around $3.50 to $5.50 per square foot, depending on its quality. This cost includes the material, inflation blowers and controls, thermal liner, auxiliary backup system, doors, and heating system. It does not include foundations, the tennis courts, and lighting.

The main advantages of a bubble, other than initial price, are that power requirements for lighting can be lower and that it can be deflated during summer seasons when members prefer to play outdoors. The main disadvantages are possible collapse because of high velocity winds or heavy snows, limited useful life, and the annual seasonal costs of erection and removal, which generally amount to about 2% of gross revenues.

The courts themselves are generally spacious and well lit. Heated in the winter and air-conditioned in the summer, indoor courts provide nearly perfect, climate-controlled environments for play. It is this very ideal setting that has encouraged the development of the indoor/outdoor combination tennis club.

In areas of the country where seasonal variations produce moderate summer temperatures and cold or rainy winters, the indoor/outdoor club has become popular. But even in regions that are sunny year-round, the option of indoor tennis courts is attractive to members who prefer a more controlled environment where they do not have to deal with wind, humidity, glare, or direct rays from the sun.

Most indoor/outdoor clubs have permanent structures to cover some of their courts. The air bubble construction, however, is utilized by those clubs that only want to feature indoor play during the winter months; the bubbles can then be taken down in summer, thus providing members with seasonally variable playing environments.

Expert advice is required for the complex subject of court construction. The basic factors to consider include desired speed (slow court or fast court), slope, porous or nonporous construction, and type and color of surface. Cost can vary greatly from one type to another and within geographic areas. Certain types tend to be preferred. The porous or pervious construction permits water to filter through the surface and includes clay, grass, dirt, and specially prepared crushed aggregate types.

Initial cost and maintenance are prime considerations. The most popular impervious types are asphalt or concrete. Major considerations are proper preparation of the site: subgrade materials; drainage; base course or foundation; and the upper tier, or leveling, course. The top surface may be cushioned or noncushioned.

Other factors that affect the selection of tennis court type and surface include climate, maintenance, resurfacing cost, hardness, ball skid length, effect on ball spin, uniformity of ball bounce, color, drying time after rain, effects of humidity, and control of stains. The U.S. Tennis Association has published extensive information on this subject including rating system guidelines. These publications should be required reading for anyone dealing with this subject.

Indoor and outdoor court lighting is also a highly specialized subject. A variety of types are available with different initial costs and associated operating expenses. A major consideration is the level of light desired. Other factors include uniformity, glare, shadow effects, and the mixing of natural light.

Outdoor and indoor courts have different requirements for quantity of light and types of systems. The first question is whether to light outdoor courts at all because nighttime play may only be popular in certain climates. Outdoor lighting is usually a problem with surrounding residences because of its effects on views and privacy. Outdoor courts are lighted by floodlights or indirect fluorescent systems. Floodlights can be incandescent or quartz mercury vapor, tungsten, halogen, metal halide, or high pressure sodium lamps. Fluorescent systems, which have become quite popular, cause the fewest visual problems for players but are generally higher priced.

Many of the same systems are used for indoor lighting, but the most popular is an indirect system whereby quartz or mercury vapor lamps are directed to a light-reflective ceiling cover. This system eliminates hot spots and assures the players of clear vision when looking up to serve or to deliver an overhead return. Some systems combine fluorescent or semidirect with an upward or reflected source that capitalizes on the advantages of both types.

Indoor courts will require heat, ventilation and, in some parts of the country, air conditioning. The tendency is to establish a lower minimum temperature in winter (e.g., 60 degrees) and a higher maximum temperature in summer (e.g., 75 degrees) for greatest energy efficiency.

Tennis courts are ideally in units of 60 feet by 120 feet. When they are placed in groups of two or more, space between courts may be reduced to the point where average size may be 54 feet by 120 feet, which is a savings of 720 square feet or 10%. Courts should not be placed less than 10 feet apart because players on adjacent courts can interfere with each other's game.

Outdoor courts should be placed close to north-south axis to reduce the effect of the sun on the tennis game. However, the configuration of the site may be the controlling factor. In any event, the analyst should be aware of this situation when comparing one club to another for qualitative rating purposes.

The classic tennis image conjures up idyllic pictures of quiet repose in the lap of luxury. It is a concept that has easily lent itself to the resort vacation. Now, as more and more people seek to combine the luxury vacation with their favorite recreational activities, tennis vacation resorts are booming. In 1978 roughly 200 U.S. tennis resorts were available to vacationers. Today that figure has increased by more than 50% to well over 300 resorts.[1]

Not only are more resorts available, but they have become increasingly sophisticated in catering to the specific needs of tennis players. To compete successfully, a tennis resort must offer much more than a handful of tennis courts. To survive, especially in the highly competitive Sunbelt regions, a resort must carve out its own unique niche to lure tennis-playing clientele. Increasingly, tennis resorts must promise something extraordinary not only on the court but off the court as well.

A hotel or motel that is going to promote itself by offering tennis should have at least two courts. But if the facility is positioning itself against prestigious resorts, a minimum of eight courts is really required. Other elements that comprise a distinguished tennis resort are the quality of the tennis facilities, the instructional programs, the availability of courts, the balance of players who make up the clientele, the active presence of tennis personalities, game arranging services, and a friendly and helpful staff.

Tennis resorts are more than tennis sites: They are vacation centers, and consequently their accommodations and complementary amenities must be on an equal or better order than typical tennis clubs. In some cases, the off-court elements of a facility are developed to such an extent as to cross-classify the tennis resort as a health spa. These facilities not only offer extensive tennis facilities but also specialize in complete diagnostic health testing and preventive medicine. Health spas are discussed to a greater extent later in this chapter.

Court Clubs

During the boom years of tennis, tennis clubs were the dominant type of court facility; they rarely offered other types of court sports. Anyone interested in playing squash or handball had to search for courts, usually at the local YMCA or at a more exclusive squash club.

Consumer tastes in fitness have grown more diverse, however, and the focus of court club activity has shifted over the past ten years. Tennis is still the dominant activity at a tennis club, but now many tennis clubs also offer other court games—particularly racquetball, handball, and squash.

It was the popularity of racquetball—the game itself coupled with its space and cost efficiencies—that prompted the huge development of court clubs. A racquetball court is only 20 by 40 feet, one ninth the size of a standard tennis court. Therefore, a racquetball club requires much less land than a tennis club. Racquetball entrepreneurs quickly capitalized on the game's economic advantages, and racquet clubs became the ideal fitness developments for urban settings. In fact, racquetball facilities once accounted for a significant percentage of court clubs and actually started to define the court club category.

Racquetball facilities as single-purpose structures, however, soon faced the same pressures of changing consumer tastes that prompted tennis clubs to expand their athletic offerings. Court club members wanted to be surrounded by much more than simply four walls and a high ceiling. In order to survive, court clubs have had to provide a full complement of amenities. Today's court club is likely to feature a combination of racquetball and squash courts, a weight training center, an aerobic exercise studio, a lounge, pro shop, men's and women's locker rooms, spa area, nursery, and snack bar.

Court clubs range in size from 4 courts to over 30, with a typical facility averaging 10 courts. The smaller court clubs have a competitive disadvantage; they cannot take advantage of the potential income generated by additional club services, such as those provided by a pro shop, food and beverage service, tournaments, and so forth. These separate profit centers can produce up to 25% of the gross revenue.

In constructing court clubs, top quality materials should be used to extend the life cycle of the facility. Proper lighting, ventilation, and surface finishes are also important considerations. Constructing the courts below ground level may help to reduce heating and air conditioning costs. Glass backwall systems facilitate tournament viewing and are used for marketing. Most glass wall systems can include side walls as well as back walls. These walls are movable, which allows conversion of courts to other uses. For example, a racquetball court can convert to one squash-sized court and also provide additional space for aerobics or gymnasium uses.

Another technique is to utilize mezzanine systems that can convert underutilized courts into two productive units. The new "rooms" can be used for aerobic dance classes, weight rooms, tanning rooms, day care, or office space. Certain contractors sell prefabricated converter units that are temporary (i.e., nonstructural) and thereby offer the added benefits of potential investment tax credits and a shorter life for depreciation purposes. In some jurisdictions installation of these systems may not even require a building permit.

Racquet clubs designed as single-use facilities are not favorably viewed by prospective lenders and investors. Therefore, designing elements prior to construction that will facilitate conversion to other uses, such as retail, office, or warehouse space, may positively influence lenders in evaluating loan requests. Such design elements as steel overhead door lintels with knockout panels, structural systems with nonbearing court walls that can be removed, and mercury vapor lighting will make conversion to other commercial or industrial uses more financially feasible.

Multisport Athletic Clubs

Like the court club, a multisport athletic club offers playing courts for racquetball, handball, squash, and, in some instances, even tennis. The multisport athletic club emphasizes its weight training centers and aerobic facilities as well as additional opportunities for basketball, swimming, indoor track, and gymnastic programs. No one activity is dominant. Instead, these clubs provide variety in exercise and fitness.

The growth of the multisport facility is relatively new. A decade ago such combinations of sport activities were only found in YMCAs and other community centers. As a result, the facilities are either recently constructed or exist in recently renovated spaces. The design (interior and exterior) and finishes are planned to meet contemporary tastes and standards.

In a few cases, particularly in older clubs, the construction and design of the club will limit its programs and offerings. For example, pools may be small (less than 50 feet in length), and treadmills are used as a substitute for an indoor running track.

The multifaceted nature of the sports club's activities also promotes a social orientation. Restaurants, lounges, and snack bars are often integral features. Today's multisport athletic club seeks to serve as a focal point for its members' social lives. Extra services and programs—such as excursions, parties, tournaments, leagues, organized children's activities, babysitting services, lectures and classes—are common and expand the club's usefulness.

The construction and design points discussed earlier for tennis and court clubs also apply to the multisport facility that includes these activities; however, there are other unique construction concerns for the multisport facility, primarily in pool and gymnasium design.

A gymnasium is not a direct profit center for a club, but it can be an effective tool for member retention. For an example, a full-sized, 94 by 50 foot, gymnasium court can be utilized for basketball league play, or it can be divided into two smaller courts to accommodate half-court open play or different gymnasium programs such as volleyball or aerobics.

A tactic used by clubs that do not have gymnasium space available but still want to offer gymnasium programs to members is to offer basketball and/or volleyball games in racquetball courts. A crossbreed of racquetball and basketball, called racquet-court basketball, attracts basketball players and helps fill idle courts. Racquetball courts are easily converted into two-on-two basketball courts by simply adding convertible baskets to the courts. The baskets can be flipped up into the observation area when the court space is needed for racquet games.[2]

Wallyball is a version of volleyball that is played in a racquetball court. Like racquet-court basketball, it was designed with the express purpose of utilizing empty racquetball courts. The game is suitable for teams of two to four persons and is played much like volleyball except the ball can be hit off the side walls and ceilings of the court. The walls keep shots in play that would otherwise be lost, and players get longer rallies and better cardiovascular workouts.[3]

Fitness industry observers predict that swimming pools are fast becoming required equipment for the multisport club. The rapid growth in popularity of aqua aerobics and lap swimming spells profitability for the club with a proper-sized pool. According to IRSA's industry data, multisport athletic clubs with pools had an average of 672 more members than their dry counterparts, and their average total revenues were over 50% higher.[4]

The addition of a swimming pool appears to be a priority among the capital expenditures that existing clubs are considering. For example, IRSA found that 29% of the racquetball/squash clubs and 22% of the multisport clubs without pools are considering adding an indoor pool. Adding outdoor pools, however, is far less popular, with 9% of the racquetball/squash clubs and 4% of the multisport clubs without pools responding favorably to this option.[5]

Swimming pools should be used by clubs as marketing tools. Potential members who are hesitant about exercise can be introduced to a satisfying fitness regimen in water. Swimming and other forms of water exercise, such as aqua aerobics, are not as stressful to the body as other types of exercise workouts. This characteristic is particularly attractive to the over age 50 crowd.

A club should follow five basic steps to ensure its optimal pool design:[6]

- *Step #1.* Evaluate the uses of the pool: What is the purpose of the pool and what kind of pool will be most appealing to the club's members and prospective members? Will the pool be strictly a lap pool or should it be designed to accommodate family programs and diving programs? A useful design that allows for both diving and lap or social swimming at the same time is the L-shaped swimming pool.

- *Step #2.* Evaluate the present physical capabilities of the club: Is there adequate space for a pool or will the club have to be renovated? If the pool is for year-round use, the location of the pool in relation to the rest of the club is more critical. Club members want a pool that is easily accessible from the locker rooms. A pool that is utilized for summer months only has fewer locational constraints since members don't mind walking a longer distance in their swimsuits to reach the pool.

The addition of a swimming pool to a club can increase a club's membership by hundreds of people. The club considering a pool as an added amenity must therefore determine if the club can accommodate a substantial increase in membership. Are parking and locker room spaces adequate for additional traffic?

- *Step #3.* Evaluate community needs: The location of the club plays a critical role in determining the pool design. A downtown area club will attract office workers who are interested in swimming laps on their lunch hour. This club, therefore, will benefit most from a pool designed for lap swimming. A club set in the suburbs, on the other hand, will want to structure a more social swimming pool atmosphere since suburban clubs tend to be more family-oriented. This situation warrants the construction of a competition-sized pool and a child's pool.

A review of what the competition is offering in the way of swimming pools is also valuable in determining pool design. If the competition already offers recreational pools, there may be an opportunity niche to supply the community with an adult-only lap pool.

- *Step #4.* Evaluate basic options: Will this be an indoor or outdoor pool? Often clubs do not have this choice because space limitations control the decision. If the choice is available, the decision is based on factors considered in Step #1: What is the purpose of the pool? Adults concerned with a workout may prefer an indoor lap pool. Generally, however, outdoor pools are more popular for socially-oriented and family-oriented memberships. People like to swim outside and enjoy sunning around the pool. A club with a more socially-oriented adult membership may even want to consider a small outdoor, adult-only type of pool that has restaurant and bar service.

Most such pool designs are only practical for clubs located in year-round temperate climates. Clubs that do not enjoy year-round warm weather, however, can still offer an outdoor pool by utilizing bubble technology. Although keeping a bubble over a pool for eight to nine months is more energy intensive, costs tend to even out as energy expenditures are minimal for the three to five months that the bubble is down. Local contractors can provide energy cost estimates for alternate designs.

- *Step #5.* Evaluate future pool needs: What will be the function of the pool five years from now? Future considerations must be incorporated into the design of the pool. A club may determine that present needs are for a lap pool. In terms of construction, a consistent depth is more useful for a lap pool; a pool with a deep end is more popular for general swimming activities and is necessary for diving. For the future, however, management should be aware that needs may shift to include competitive activities, water exercise programs, and scuba diving and lifesaving classes. The pool that is designed strictly for lap swimming will soon find itself outdated and in a poor competitive position because these new activities require a deep end. Long-term planning up-front, though more costly and time consuming, would avoid such a scenario. Future needs are assessed in a market feasibility analysis, which is discussed in Chapter 7.

Storefront Operations

Storefront operations are small-scale enterprises emphasizing a single fitness activity. Included in the storefront operation category are aerobic fitness studios, weight training centers, and body building gyms. The operations have low overhead and small space requirements. Convenience is a key factor to their success. As a result, they are found in leased quarters in a variety of pre-existing, convenient, heavily-trafficked locales: office buildings, malls, above and below street level stores, and shops. These types of clubs rarely locate in a dedicated structure. The appraisal of a storefront operation is essentially a business valuation.

Aerobic fitness studios feature aerobic dance exercises, that is, exercise routines that are choreographed and set to music. Aerobic dance was originated by Jacki Sorensen in 1969 as an exercise program for Air Force wives. The program quickly grew in popularity and moved into the private sector. Jacki Sorensen's Aerobic Dancing studios sprang up across the country along with an offshoot chain program, Jazzercise.[7] Today, in addition to the national chain operations, there are numerous independent ventures.

The low start-up and maintenance costs make aerobic studios attractive investments for many fitness entrepreneurs. The no-frills start-up usually opens in leased space with little more than a sound system and instructors. Locker rooms, if available, are kept basic and small; spas are usually not featured at all. Many studios have made more elaborate investments, and these studios are the ones that are more likely to ride out the shifts in consumer demand.

Choreographed exercise routines are the backbone of the aerobics studio. However, as consumer tastes are diversifying, studios are finding that they need to provide complementary amenities, such as weight equipment and strength training programs, to keep their customers satisfied.

In addition, many studios also feature a small retail area where customers can purchase the latest fashions in exercise wear and accessories. These in-house profit centers operate like the tennis and racquet club pro shops and allow the fitness studio to capitalize on all aspects of the activity.

Expanded offerings and add-on profit centers, though, are not enough to make an aerobics studio successful; today especially, there is grave medical concern regarding the increasing number of aerobic injuries. A 1986 survey among aerobic students and instructors found that 43% of the students and 76% of the instructors suffered injuries.[8] How well a fitness studio responds to these market factors may very well determine its future success.

Lack of quality instruction is one of the first reasons cited for aerobic injuries. A studio's name is built on its instructors, and poor instructors can do irreparable harm to a studio's reputation. Until recently there was no regulation or certification standards in the aerobic industry. Growing public concern, though, has prompted efforts at industry self-regulation. Industry trade groups now offer instructor training programs and certification exams. A set of criteria on which aerobic instructors can be evaluated is being established.

A healthier approach to aerobic exercise is advocated by both consumer and medical groups. The philosophy of "go for the burn" is no longer acceptable. Research reveals that workouts that are less intense can still be beneficial. The American College of Obstetricians and Gynecologists is one of the many associations that have issued guidelines for healthier aerobic programs.

Many studios now incorporate a range of exercise programs. The newer and allegedly healthier low-impact and non-impact classes are given equal, if not more, time than the "traditional" high-impact classes.

Hydroaerobics (water exercises) are also growing in popularity, but for the most part the classes are only available at multipurpose sport facilities. This activity may very well represent a future source of competition for the fitness studio.

A second frequent cause of aerobic injuries is the studio floor. Unyielding floor surfaces have been cited for causing shin splints, twisted ankles, sore arches, sore calves, and overall body shock. Aerobic exercise routines, therefore, require floor surfaces that will cushion the impact of the aerobic exerciser's jumps and provide proper surface traction. A number of floor systems have been developed specifically for the aerobics industry. These resilient floating floors offer top surfaces in both hardwood and carpeting. Their expense, however, makes them prohibitive for many facilities. Often studios, moving into pre-existing buildings, will simply lay carpeting over the structure's original concrete floor. This design is very deceptive because although it looks as if the floor will absorb the impact of a jump, it really has no cushion.

The choice between hardwood and carpeting opens up other maintenance and operation questions. Hardwood floor surfaces are easier to maintain, but they require mats for floor exercises. A carpeted exercise area, on the other hand, does not need additional equipment such as floor mats, but it can hold odors, requires more work to clean, and has a shorter economic life.

Aside from a studio's floor design and the quality of its instructors, several other secondary factors contribute to a facility's success. Customers want spaciousness when they are working out, and they look for a studio that presents a bright, light, and airy environment. Even a small studio, faced with space restrictions, can give the illusion of spaciousness through the use of mirrors and high ceilings. A light-colored decor also contributes to the appearance of spaciousness. The exercise area should be well-ventilated and cool—75 degrees or below.

Weight training centers are a product of the high-tech strength training revolution of the 1970s. The high-tech training center offers access to a circuit workout that the home exerciser cannot afford. The equipment itself, as it becomes more and more computerized, is the driving force behind the rapid growth of these centers.

The equipment in a high-tech training center may include computerized rowers, cycles, stair climbers, and ladders that provide detailed workout information. Some equipment allows users to program their workout, for example, to take a three-mile jog in the country, complete with sound effects. Other machines pit exercisers against a computer. Large video screens enable clubs to mount races between several members who are using the same type of equipment. Another piece of equipment will actually talk an exerciser through the workout routine. As the above examples indicate, the weight training center has numerous marketing programs that can be developed because of its computerized exercise facilities.

The majority of weight training centers in today's market, however, are not so technologically developed. The basic training center provides an assortment of free weights and standard resistance and variable resistance machines. Some centers will provide substantial aerobic conditioning equipment as well. Body builders' gyms have an even more basic approach. The traditional gym focuses primarily on providing a good complement of free weights in an almost Spartan-like environment.

But no matter what type of equipment is featured, the training center area needs to be spacious and arranged with traffic flow in mind. Similar or complementary types of equipment should be grouped together, and training circuits should flow in order of use. A typical circuit arranges machines so that the workout begins with larger muscle groups and proceeds to smaller muscle groups. A random arrangement only creates confusion and traffic congestion. Adequate space between machines should accommodate equipment users, those waiting to use the equipment, and flow-through traffic. Free weights should be stored in racks or stands and not scattered across the training area.

The extent of a center's offerings is often limited by its physical size; most centers can only provide 1 to 1½ circuits. A room measuring 1,500 to 2,000 square feet can adequately accommodate one full circuit (12 machines) of Nautilus-type equipment. An entire facility can be housed in a space measuring between 3,500 and 5,000 square feet, an area smaller than the space required for one tennis court.[9]

Wood or vinyl is the typical floor surface for weight rooms, although the trend in the newer high-tech training centers is to use carpeting. Whichever floor surface is utilized by the training center, the floor foundation needs to be level. Training centers located in older buildings often face warped wooden floors or settling foundations. Uneven floors can create a serious problem for a facility because weight equipment requires an exceptionally level base.

Profit Centers

One of the newest trends in project developments is to integrate health and fitness facilities as add-on profit centers. As market competition heats up, more and more firms are realizing the profit potential and marketing value of in-house fitness centers.

Nowhere is the profit center trend more evident than in the hotel and lodging industry. Hotel health clubs are one of the most rapidly growing types of profit centers. In many large cities, a full service health club is now the mark of a first-class business travelers' hotel.

Another type of profit center that is experiencing rapid growth is the hospital-based fitness facility. A hospital-based fitness center can enhance the hospital's image in a community. The hospital is regarded no longer as just treating illnesses but as preventing illnesses and maintaining wellness.

The most important factor in establishing a profit center is to determine the center's overall purpose in relation to its parent facility. For example, a small hotel fitness facility could function strictly as an additional amenity for guests and would require a minimum investment on the part of the developer. These clubs operate on a relatively small scale, offering exercise bikes, some free weights, a few resistance machines, and a swimming pool.

On the other hand, a hotel fitness club could be designed to be a more comprehensive life-style center with the explicit purposes of enhancing the hotel's marketability and generating additional income. Such a club requires a defined focus, more extensive design considerations, and a larger dedicated space. If the focus of the health club is fitness, it should provide the basic workout needs: a swimming pool, track, aerobics areas, exercise equipment, and perhaps even racquet sport courts.

The majority of hotel health clubs are targeted to the business traveler, and fitness is the primary focus. People who exercise regularly do not like to break their exercise routine on a business trip. For the fitness-conscious traveler, the hotel that provides a full-service health club will be preferred to the hotel that has only an exercise room and perhaps a swimming pool. This marketing factor extends beyond the single business traveler and may affect meeting and convention planning.

The hotel fitness club that is spa-oriented caters to more of a resort/relaxation-seeking clientele. Pampering treatments are the primary features: body wraps and massages, steam rooms, whirlpools, healthful diets, and some exercise equipment.

Before the investment in a fitness center—as a profit center—is made, the feasibility of the center must be assessed. Many projects can easily become a drain on its parent establishment if more members are required than can be realistically expected. It is unlikely the hotel guests alone will make an in-house health club profitable. A hotel is, therefore, well advised to open its doors to outside membership, particularly to attract more patrons during business hours, weekends, and holidays.

If the club is open to the general public, the hotel must determine a fee structure. Will there be one fee structure for both hotel guests and community residents or will charges differ? A general rule of thumb is that a center should generate $40 per square foot from 70% of its user fee revenues.[10]

Spa Clubs

A new class of fitness facilities is emerging on the fitness scene. At present their numbers are small; however, the standard of their amenities is certain to have a competitive impact in the marketplace.

Spa clubs are health clubs with an additional twist—they combine the fitness benefits of a health club membership with the luxury of a European vacation spa. These facilities are service driven; their high standard of personalized service and pampering is based on the ideals of member service, wellness, fitness, and stress management.

Spas have a long-standing tradition in Europe, but in the United States they have had the image of being affordable only by the rich. The notion of being pampered generally conflicted with the American work ethic heritage.[11]

Spas began to be accepted on the American scene as vacation resorts or "fat farms," but they were still in the domain of the rich. As American cultural values and traditions evolved, the image of a spa, and its potential as a vacation alternative, also evolved. Spa vacations have now moved into the affluent American life-style. With the emergence of the spa club, the advantages of a spa vacation are available to members on an everyday basis.

The spa club serves as a comprehensive wellness center for its guests. Members join this type of facility not just to have an exercise outlet, but also to incorporate a balanced life-style that focuses on developing the whole person. Spa clubs offer a variety of ways to obtain relief from the stresses and strains of urban life beyond the limits of aerobic classes and weight machines.

For many spa clubs, their prime market is "not so fit" women between 30 and 50 years of age. These women choose a spa club membership rather than a regular health club membership for the spa's specialized services and pampered relaxation, therapeutic treatments, and shelter from the glaring eyes of narcissistic "jocks" that are found in many faster-paced fitness centers.

A tranquil decor is essential for instilling an appropriate atmosphere of inner peace. Subdued lighting, rich carpeting, inviting furniture, classical music, and fine art are the usual attributes that first greet the member upon entering a spa club. The mood is designed to dispel any feelings of tension and anxiety.

The spa and massage facilities are the critical features differentiating spa clubs from health clubs. Most spa clubs will offer a variety of therapeutic equipment and techniques such as Japanese therapy pools, carbonated mineral baths, Italian Fango mud treatments, herbal steam, and seaweed body-wraps and brush treatments.

Massage programs include underwater deep massage; Swedish, Trager, Esalen and Shiatsu body massages; myotherapy, a form of muscle relaxation through intense, direct pressure; and aromatherapy, a relaxation treatment which involves the use of intense, natural scented oils.

Spa treatments are an integral part of a spa club's program, but the latest in cardiovascular conditioning and weight equipment are also typical spa club offerings. These clubs generally boast a variety of state-of-the-art rowers, exercise cycles, treadmills and life-cycle machines. Their exercise studios provide aerobic, yoga, and stretch classes. To complete its offerings, many clubs will also hold classes and programs in wellness, nutrition, and stress management.

Establishing a spa club requires a different operating philosophy than what normally prevails at a general health club. Because a spa club is much more service/pampering oriented, it requires a larger staff to achieve a low member to staff ratio. Staffing, therefore, tends to be more expensive and requires more frequent and specialized training programs. The massage and therapeutic treatments require spa personnel to have much closer physical contact with members than what normally occurs at a general health club. For this reason, spa personnel must be highly personable and must be able to instill a strong element of trust in the spa club members.

Finally, the appearance of the club is critical. Spa clubs have a look about them that sets them apart from fitness centers. The decor needs to make a sophisticated statement that is aimed at instilling warmth and pleasing the clientele. Luxurious furnishings, artwork, fresh flowers, and fresh-smelling air are a few of the decorating techniques that help create a pleasant ambiance.

Niche Clubs

Many health clubs have achieved success by differentiating themselves with a niche strategy. A niche strategy essentially involves discerning a small, unique segment of the market that is not being served and exploiting that unmet need. Successful niche strategies in the fitness industry have focused on location and/or servicing special audiences.

Airport health clubs are emerging in some of the major airports in the country.[12] The clubs position themselves to offer travelers, particularly busy business executives, an oasis of comfort in the midst of a tense environment. Now travelers can fit in a workout between airline connections or during unexpected delays. The amenities the clubs offer are especially geared to meet the travelers' needs. Figuring that most travelers have everything packed, the clubs provide valet pressing, towels, lotions, sundries, safe-deposit boxes, workout clothes, and bathrobes. For the business executive, some clubs provide private office space complete with a desk, a personal computer, a phone, photocopying facilities, and courier services.

In addition to such customized amenities, the airport health clubs offer typical fitness club and spa services. Most clubs offer weight equipment, treadmills, a swimming pool, steam room, massage services, and a nap room.

The clientele is primarily working women who are looking for a safe environment when traveling alone and who hate to break up their workout routine because of business trips. The clubs limit the number of total guests to avoid overcrowding, but the clubs will accept reservations made in advance from those travelers who know their flight schedules.

Another successful niche club is a franchise that targets people 50 and older.[13] These clubs are relying on the fact that typical health clubs are primarily geared to a young audience and are not addressing the unique needs of an over-50 clientele.

Because cohort groups tend to feel more comfortable in the company of their peers, older people feel more relaxed and at ease in an exercise environment that is designed for their abilities. The exercise clubs that target the elderly have exercise classes that stress working at one's own pace. The music that accompanies the workouts is from the 1930s and 1940s. The music from a member's adolescence is not the music of today's youth.

Research findings indicate that companionship, as well as exercise, is important to people 50 and over. To meet this need, the clubs provide social gathering areas with tables, chairs, and vending machines.

A final differentiating factor used by the over-50 clubs is their fee structure. Rather than long-term fees, the clubs use a month-to-month payment schedule that is a more appropriate program because of the fixed income status of most of the club members.

Another overlooked market segment that was successfully tapped by a fitness franchise is overweight women.[14] Just as older people do not feel comfortable in a trendy health club setting, large women feel embarrassed exercising in the "body beautiful" environment.

Clubs targeted at the larger woman cater to their customers' need to feel feminine and accepted. The clubs do not push the "thin is in" concept. They stress that it is acceptable to be overweight; and their programming emphasizes fitness, not weight reduction. Their philosophy is extended to encompass all aspects of the club—including the instructors. Many franchises hire only overweight aerobic teachers because their overweight customers feel defeated when taught by svelte instructors.

The club's concept has also been extended to include profit center boutiques. The club carries its own line of leotards, tights, and exercise clothing designed specifically for the larger woman.

Niche fitness clubs have also expanded into the children's market. A national franchise offers exercise classes for children as young as five months old.[15] The franchise does not stop with an exercise club; the youngsters are also plied with videotapes, toys, and clothing. Some multisport clubs, marketing their family-oriented approaches, are establishing special children's programs. A few fitness equipment manufacturers are producing exercise machines especially designed for children.

Miscellaneous Services

As mentioned at the beginning of this chapter, fitness clubs have added a number of amenities to keep pace in a competitive market. In addition to the array of fitness activities, fitness accessories, and spa features, clubs are adding profit centers in the form of health counseling and motivation services. These services are commonly referred to as wellness programs.

The wellness program offers the club member counseling on nutrition, exercise, and general life-style habits. It also works as a motivational tool to keep the member on his or her exercise track.

The wellness director will establish an exercise program for the member. The program will begin with an exercise pretest to measure the member's physical abilities and to assess limitations. Once the base point is determined, the wellness director sets up a strengthening regimen for the member to follow.

A variation on this theme is the one-on-one training technique. Fitness counselors accompany club members through an exercise circuit geared to the individual's fitness goals. The member tends to work harder when instructed by a counselor and given encouragement. Users of the one-on-one service usually pay an additional fee on an hourly basis. The club facilitates scheduling of one-on-one sessions and screens the qualifications of instructors.

Despite the controversy over the negative long-term effects on skin, one of the fastest growing profit centers in the fitness industry is tanning services. They are a natural addition to the fitness operation because today's culture values a tanned body for the healthful and active image it conveys.

A tanning system can be easily installed and operated, it does not require much space, and it yields high profit margins. As a consequence, tanning booths or beds are being added to all types of fitness operations, from the small aerobic studio to the multipurpose sports club.

The most essential considerations in operating a tanning system are health and safety factors. Before a person can use the tanning service, a brief medical report must be completed and a liability waiver signed. A reputable operation should inform users of possible health hazards connected with artificial tanning and should provide instruction on the safe operation of the tanning equipment. A safe tanning program should always start with limited exposure and gradually build up to no more than a 25- to 30-minute session. Most tanning systems are operated with a timing device that is activated by the user, but set by the operator.

The club must maintain high sanitation standards since tanning is an activity that can easily support the spread of disease. The tanning bed should be sanitized after every session. The club should also provide cups to protect the eyes.

To embellish their tanning services, many clubs will offer complimentary sundries, such as body lotion. Furthermore, to make the tanning session more enjoyable most clubs provide fans and radio headsets. Tanning rooms are sometimes given exotic names, such as St. Thomas, Nassau, or Jamaica.

Another service clubs are adding is fitness testing. Many members are eager to learn their proportions of muscle, body fat, and water. Several different testing procedures are available, including, in order of increasing accuracy and expense, calipers, electronic scanning, and water flotation techniques. This service is often combined with a wellness program to counsel members regarding proper diet and exercise routines. Fitness testing helps members to establish fitness goals and to gauge progress.

On a more traditional level, many recreational facilities generate additional profit through lessons and classes. These services often complement a club's main activities, for example, tennis or swimming lessons. Teaching services not only generate additional revenue but assist in attracting and retaining members.

The overall variety of facilities and services health clubs provide is illustrated in Table 2.1. This table summarizes the results of a survey of all clubs in the San Francisco metropolitan area. Virtually all clubs have free weights/weight machines and exercycles. Most clubs also provide sauna/steam facilities and other types of cardiovascular machines in addition to exercycles. Close to 40% of all clubs include swimming pools, racquetball/handball courts, and gymnasiums yet very few feature tennis courts and tracks. The tendency of clubs to provide personal trainers, aerobics classes, and fitness testing/nutritional counseling is very high. A moderate percentage of clubs include child supervision, massage, and food and beverage services for their members.

Table 2.1　Survey of Health Club Facilities and Services

	Number	Percentage
Total Clubs Surveyed	149	100 %
Clubs with Identified Facilities		
Freeweights/Weight Machines	147	98.7%
Exercycles	147	98.7%
Sauna/Steam	129	86.6%
Other Cardiovascular Machines	96	64.4%
Pool (excluding jaccuzzis)	60	42.3%
Racquetball/Handball Courts	55	40.3%
Basketball/Volleyball Courts	63	36.9%
Tennis Courts	24	16.1%
Track	9	6.0%
Clubs with Identified Services		
Personal Trainers	135	90.6%
Aerobics Classes	121	81.2%
Fitness Testing/Nutritional Counseling	117	78.5%
Child Supervision	73	49.0%
Massage	73	49.0%
Prepared Food/Beverage Service	57	38.3%

This survey encompassed all clubs in the five county San Francisco Metropolitan Area. The results exclude YMCAs and JCCs from the tabulations.

Source: "1988 Guide to Health Clubs," *City Sports* (San Francisco Edition, February, 1988) pp. 37-43.

Overall Facility Evaluations

The health club proprietor should always seek new means to improve profitability. Two of the most basic areas to examine are the physical facilities and the club's services.

Facility expansion requires careful analysis because it tends to be capital intensive. An obvious example is whether or not to add a swimming pool. Deriving greater usage, and revenue, out of existing facilities also is valid consideration. Could an underutilized racquetball court become more profitable as an aerobics or fitness room?

Similarly, club operators can respond to changing market demand by adding services. Often, adding services does not require extensive capital investment, and it can be accomplished more quickly than physical improvements.

Club operators also must recognize unprofitable areas of operation. While some facilities and services are necessary to retain and attract members in the face of competition, other facilities and services may be cut back with a net operational gain. Gathering information for this type of cost/benefit analysis includes carefully observing facilities' usage, investigating competition, reviewing accounting statements, and discussing likes and dislikes with members and applicants. The astute club manager will stay abreast of all these operational facets.

Exhibit 2.2   Health Club Exterior Photographs

Freestanding Class C Multisport Club

Storefront health club, as part of a neighborhood shopping center

Exhibit 2.3 Freestanding Tennis Building Photographs

Class C and S tennis building exterior

Freestanding tennis building interior

Exhibit 2.4   Club Interior Photographs

Interior swimming pool as part of a multisport club

Typical spa area as part of a multisport club

Exhibit 2.5   Club Interior Photographs

Typical weight training room

Health club snack bar

Site
Considerations

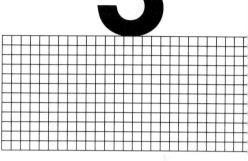

The health/fitness industry is a young industry, and, as a consequence, successful sites have often been located by reviewing a predecessors' trials and errors. As a general rule, however, potentially profitable sites are identified after a thorough examination of location, accessibility, size, shape, zoning restrictions, competition, and land prices.

To assess these factors accurately, the appraiser needs to have a broad understanding of the local physical fitness market and the characteristics of competing facilities. Analysis of surrounding land uses and alternate locations are also critical to the assessment.

Many costly errors in development have been made because obvious details were ignored. For example, a common mistake is situating outdoor tennis courts without first consulting community rulings on night lighting. Substantial community opposition to night lighting in certain areas is a major constraint to the utilization of land for outdoor courts. These restrictions become especially debilitating in areas where the evening may be the most desirable time to play, for instance, in the hot Southwest.

Another example is the lack of planning in locating parking areas in reference to a club's entrance. Club members attending intense one hour workouts do not necessarily want to include a long trek from their car to the club as a part of their routine. Fitness is still a convenience industry, and a club will have a problem if members have to park too far away.[1]

Adjusting an original design to consider acoustics is another consideration that is often overlooked. Existing structures may need to be reinforced to prevent sound reverberations in the structural system between floors and between offices.[2] This consideration is particularly important when clubs locate in buildings with other uses.

Obviously, these examples illustrate that extreme care must be exercised in the development stage.

Location

Location is crucial to the success of a health/fitness facility. The health club should locate close to the market it will serve, and to a great extent the location of a club defines its target market.

The deluxe tennis club should locate in an upper income suburb to take advantage of adequate land area and a population that can afford to support the club. The fitness studio that presents a basic no-frills image and fee structure is better situated in a working class to middle class area.

When physical placement and club image are not complementary, the developer runs the risk of increasing the barriers to reaching the target market. A myriad of psychological variables can influence the attractiveness of a club's location.

For example, a location on a certain side of town could create social barriers. While some clubs situated in warehouse districts have been successful, others have had problems attracting members. Players are hesitant to travel at night in industrial districts that they deem unsafe. In addition, a security problem can exist for the club in terms of potential vandalism and burglary. On the other hand, a white collar business park setting suggests a corporate clientele for a nearby club. Such a location, however, may inhibit membership of noncorporate individuals shopping for health clubs.

Another consideration in locating a health/fitness facility is travel time requirements. A site in an outlying district may be low-priced and spacious, but it may also meet resistance from potential members because of excessive travel time requirements. Research indicates that there is definitely a specific distance beyond which people will not travel to come to a club. The findings from a 1984 study, commissioned by the International Racquet Sports Association (IRSA), are represented in Table 3.1. The table shows the distance necessary to generate from 50% to 90% of a club's total membership. As can be seen, 60% of the membership of the average club live within 6.6 miles of the facility; 80% live within 8.6 miles of the club; and beyond 13 miles, membership is negligible.

Establishing a health club facility in a projected growth area has special considerations. Growth projections need to be thoroughly evaluated. Will an adequate target population move into the area to support the club? Will this movement occur within a feasible time frame? Existing and future road systems also need to be reviewed. Does the city planning office anticipate shifts in main travel routes that may isolate the club?

The proximity of other noncompetitive, mutually supportive commercial and recreational businesses also contribute to club siting considerations. A club utilizing this placement strategy capitalizes on the spillover effect one establishment has on another facility. Consider combining an aerobics dance studio with a weight lifting center or situating a racquetball club near a community swimming pool. The strategy can be extended beyond compatible sports facilities to encompass other complementary entertainment-oriented or commercial establishments. For instance, locating a health club near restaurants, movie theatres, or a shopping center could create beneficial spillover effects. The aforementioned strategic locales all enhance a club's appeal while offering members a convenient way to eat, shop, and/or socialize before or after a workout.

Accessibility

Primary site locations are in main commercial areas. Such settings are highly attractive because they are clearly visible, easily accessed, and convenient for large audience segments. Some of the best examples are adjacent to freeway interchanges. Of course, the developer will pay a premium price for these advantages.

Sites situated outside main commercial areas in secondary locales are still desirable location alternatives. While visibility and exposure are certainly positive benefits, they are not necessary requirements for the

Table 3.1 Distance Members Live from Clubs Based on a Profile of 22 Clubs

Category	Total Clubs	6 Racquet Clubs	7 Tennis Clubs	9 Multisport Clubs
Total Members	29,363	8,870	6,566	13,927
Average Members Per Club	1,335	1,478	938	1,547
Average Distance to Generate % of Membership (in miles)				
50%	5.6 miles	5.5 miles	5.9 miles	5.5 miles
60%	6.6 miles	7.0 miles	6.7 miles	6.2 miles
70%	7.4 miles	7.9 miles	7.6 miles	7.0 miles
80%	8.6 miles	9.0 miles	8.6 miles	8.2 miles
90%	11.2 miles	12.4 miles	12.2 miles	9.5 miles

Source: Ron Lawrence, "Club Location—Setting Your Sights on the Right Site," *Club Business* (Brookline: IRSA, April 1984), p. 24.

health club facility—especially the well-marketed facility. The fitness industry does not depend upon street traffic. In addition, the lower land costs for these secondary site locations make them attractive alternatives.

Secondary settings, though, do require more attention in other areas. Development plans must take into account the relationship of the site to the street, the traffic volume on the frontage road, and the number of curb cuts. Players want clubs that do not require complicated travel routes and that they can easily reach. Provision for proper ingress and egress must be considered. Appropriate lighting for safety is critical, especially for facilities located in more rural or dimly lit areas.

New facility developments in quiet residential areas may encounter community resistance because of concerns over additional traffic the club will generate. The developer must anticipate probable travel routes and gauge such developments against community acceptance and regulations.

Size

The size requirements for a site are determined by the amenities and services the health/fitness facility will offer. In some cases, the club developer will have no control over size stipulations as they are set by local government or zoning regulations. In other cases the developers' choices of amenities will directly determine size.

The developer who wants to include a swimming pool in the facility faces considerable sizing issues that can only be approached once the purpose of the pool has been defined. Will this be a pool for dipping or one to attract the serious swimmer?

A dipping pool can be relatively small—35 feet long—but at this size it will not be much of a drawing feature for the club. The potential member looking for a quality swimming program wants a pool fitted with lap lanes long enough to provide a serious workout. To fulfill this need, the developer must consider a minimum pool length of 50 feet. A "short course" pool measures 25 yards in length and a valid Olympic-sized pool is 55 yards by 23 yards.[3]

A running track has space considerations that must be evaluated in terms of member satisfaction. A longer track is more desirable to club members because it better accommodates peak hour runner traffic and with fewer circuits to the mile it provides a less tedious and less stressful run. The absolute minimum size to consider in establishing a running track is 200 feet to provide the runner with no more than 26 laps to the mile.[4]

When sizing a running track, the developer has several economical placement alternatives to consider. Such flexibility contrasts sharply with the sizing stipulations imposed by other more rigidly established amenities, such as swimming pools or tennis courts. Whereas pools and courts have unique space requirements, indoor tracks can share space with other amenities. Tracks are often suspended above basketball or tennis courts; in other designs they have been built around equipment areas.

Clubs offering court sports have sizing considerations that must conform to game regulations. A tennis court must be 120 feet by 60 feet, which includes 21 feet from each base line to the back stop and 12 feet to each side stop from the doubles court line. Beyond meeting regulation size, however, adequate room along the sidelines and behind the base lines of courts should also be provided. The extra space helps prevent the stray balls of adjacent courts from causing frustrating interruptions. Techniques to remedy the problem when perimeter space is inadequate include hanging a net between the courts or constructing fences.

For the tennis club, depending on the number of courts and the way they are laid out, an average of about 6,250 square feet of floor area per court may be required. When many courts are placed side by side, there are savings in space between courts. Ideally, one court would require a width of 60 feet and a length of 120 feet. When courts are constructed in groups of two or more, at least 10 to 12 feet should be allowed between courts. The area per court will actually diminish as the number of courts increase, since each additional court set beside another only adds 46 to 48 feet to the width of the bank courts.

Other racquet sports, such as racquetball, handball, and squash, have much smaller court area requirements. Clubs featuring such amenities can accommodate a higher density of courts per unit of land area. The regulation dimension for racquetball/handball is 20 feet by 40 feet by 20 feet high. A squash court dimension is much smaller: 32 feet by 18½ feet. One or two squash courts can often be fitted into irregular areas remaining from a racquetball/handball development, and six squash courts can fit into the space of one tennis court.

As recreational demand shifts, many clubs remodel and convert existing features into new amenities. Often sizing problems can arise. For instance, several clubs have converted racquetball courts into aerobic or weight rooms. However, since a racquetball court is roughly 800 square feet and a complete circuit of Nautilus equipment includes 12 or more machines, the conditions in the weight room become very crowded. Nautilus Sports/Medical Industries recommends an area that is at least 2,000 square feet. This size will accommodate the 12 machines in an environment that is spacious and comfortable for the users.[5] Some clubs have redesigned their interiors to "double-deck" racquetball courts into two floors. This renovation technique avoids greater land area requirements.

Other sizing questions are raised by the extent of the clubhouse facilities. How much space will be devoted to the lounge area? to the locker room and spa? Parking requirements and setbacks are important factors that need to be studied carefully. Ample parking spaces need to be estimated to accommodate membership growth and to avoid peak-time congestion. Parking requirements for clubs usually are stipulated by local governments through zoning regulations.

Some tennis clubs examined in our research required only 1.5 acres of land for eight courts and a clubhouse. They achieved this tight ratio of 5.3 courts per acre because of minimal parking provisions and the lack of setback requirements in the local zoning ordinances. More generous ratios allot 4 to 12.5 parking spaces per court.

A final, yet perhaps the most important factor in determining size, is market demand for the facilities. A large facility may offer economies of scale, but if market demand is inadequate, the facility operating costs will simply drain an investment dry. The converse is also true. If capital investment is insufficient and a club is too small to accommodate market demand, the club could actually lose business in the face of a large, potential clientele. An overcrowded club creates frustrating situations and easily alienates its members.

Shape

Health and fitness clubs can usually be situated on a variety of property shapes without too much difficulty in design and construction. Freeway interchange remainders, sloping land within canyons, and other locations with unusual topography have been successfully utilized.

Of course certain amenities, particularly the more sizable club features, will have specific shape requirements. Indoor tennis courts typically require rectangular sites or a close variation. This design allows courts to be positioned in banks and provides the most efficient ratio of court area to land. Outdoor courts, on the other hand, can be situated on more irregularly shaped land parcels because the courts can be placed on different levels, at different angles to one another, and in other more unusual spacing arrangements. The illustration in Exhibit 3.2 is a good example of an indoor-outdoor tennis club making efficient use of an irregularly-shaped land parcel. It offers 24 courts on 7.5 acres of land.

Swimming pools are another amenity with specific shape considerations. The best and most common swimming pool shape is the rectangle. Other pool shapes—round, kidney and oval—are space-wasting configurations that are not appropriate for lap swimming.

Competition

An analysis of the competition is an essential component in any site evaluation. The initial analysis of the market environment defines the geographic boundaries of the trade area and identifies the relevant competitors. The club developer must then conduct a more in-depth inquiry: Where are the nearest competitors situated? What advantages/disadvantages do the competitions' locations have compared with the proposed site location? How do the competitions' trade areas and degrees of market penetration impact the proposed trade area and penetration estimates? Is the population base large enough to support the proposed facility and the competition?

Market feasibility research is a complex subject that is addressed in Chapter 7. The results of such a study are invaluable when attempting to select an appropriate site for a club.

Zoning

Health and fitness facilities may be situated on land zoned for commercial, industrial, or other uses. Clubs with outdoor activities have a greater range of site possibilities because they are typically found in residential areas, where land can be relatively inexpensive, as well as in other zoning districts, such as commercial and industrial areas. They usually require conditional use permits.

Indoor tennis clubs are generally found on sites zoned for commercial and industrial use, but some suburban facilities have also been placed in apartment districts under a conditional use or variance

Exhibit 3.2   Example of Site Plan for an Outdoor Tennis Club

arrangement. Racquetball clubs are typically located in industrial parks or in locations where the warehouse-type structure will have potential convertibility with a minimum of cost or difficulty for the developer. Single-purpose multisport club buildings generally are constructed in commercial zones. Aerobics and weight training centers usually locate in storefront commercial spaces, such as shopping centers, and are not directly influenced by zoning considerations.

In outlying areas clubs may situate on sites zoned for agriculture or some other holding designation. In some communities proper master planning will provide for a grouping of future land uses that will enhance utilization of the recreational project and provide benefits to the local populace. In general, low-density rural areas do not provide a sufficient market basis for recreational clubs.

Heavy industrial areas, with dense volumes of commercial vehicle traffic and industrial emissions, should be avoided. Sites with specialized sectors can be developed but do require well-planned layouts. For example, the areas under high power lines can be utilized for parking and outdoor tennis.

Land Costs

The location of a recreational project is influenced by land prices. The overall economic feasibility of a club is partially attributed to the initial land costs. A wide variation in square foot costs can be supported, depending on the potential revenue sources. A downtown club in a major metropolitan area would command a unit price many times that of the typical suburban site. In small agricultural towns outdoor clubs have cost as little as $1 per square foot of land area, while in suburban areas the range more likely may be $5 to $20 per square foot. It is preferable to make comparisons on a recreational unit factor basis such as price per court. A per court land value analysis, however, cannot be utilized unless there is sufficient land sale data from the market derived from several proposed club sites. The competitive market within the neighborhood for sites zoned for a particular use affects the land price for a project; therefore, the financial aspects of the project must be studied carefully to adjust for this requirement.

It is apparent that fewer sites will be available for clubs in urban areas in the future because of a reduction in vacant land available for use and the higher unit costs that will be required for the remaining undeveloped land. This situation already has manifested in the New York City area for tennis clubs. Although New York City, especially Manhattan, represents the extreme for almost any life-style or economic trend, it still presents a useful urban model.

According to estimates by the United States Tennis Association, the average hourly rate in New York is $65 in Manhattan and $45 in the suburbs. The court fees may be similar to those charged in other major Northeast cities, but they are nearly double the average for large cities nationwide. A court in Nashville, by comparison, goes for $25 an hour.

Despite the grossly high court fees, not to mention membership dues that can exceed $2000 for a full year, New York City tennis clubs are struggling to succeed because of a common, nationwide real estate equation: The land is more attractive and valuable to investors when used for offices, retail projects, or high-density residential buildings. Clubs featuring other racquet sports and smaller-scale amenities are not faced with such severe land restrictions because they have much higher ratios of courts or workout space per unit of land.

Site selection requires careful balancing and fine tuning. The developer must weigh land and space costs against the current and potential market demands. Site selection will also depend on the developer's position in regard to risk. There will always be successful clubs that defy all norms. For example, IRSA research uncovered a highly profitable large-scale Chicago club that is not supported at all by its immediate market area. Over 45% of the members travel more than five miles and pass two other competing clubs to reach their destination. Thus, rigid rules concerning site selection are impossible to define.

Characteristics of Market Analysis

The "Great American Shape-up" rages on: conversations boast of miles run, laps completed, and pounds pressed; lunch hours are no longer for eating but for working out; joggers can be seen running from dawn to dusk; and some fitness centers now promote 24-hour operations to service the fitness-crazed public.

The Gallup Opinion Index, presented in Chapter 1, highlights this growth in sports participation. This chapter presents a more in-depth look at the demographic characteristics of physical fitness enthusiasts. It includes a discussion of some of the tools and procedures used in analyzing demographic composition and evaluating market potential.

Demographics—A Few Statistics

The statistics in Table 4.1 reveal that, with a few exceptions, men tend to participate in sports activities more than women. Swimming is the exception in that it is not only America's favorite sport activity, but it is also an equal favorite among men and women; nearly four out of ten men and women participate in the sport. It is not surprising, in looking at the table, that the sport activities that are much more popular with men include team sports such as basketball and softball and activities such as weight training. Although the number of women participating in all activities is increasing, the majority of women favor aerobic exercise and bicycling.

Table 4.1   1986 Sports Participation

	Percentage of Participants			Number of Participants (in millions)		
Activity	Total	Men	Women	Total	Men	Women
Swimming	41	42	40	70.4	34.0	36.4
Jogging	23	25	21	39.0	20.2	18.8
Weight Training	19	26	12	31.7	20.9	10.8
Aerobics	19	7	31	32.4	5.5	26.9
Golf	12	18	7	21.0	14.4	6.6
Bowling	23	23	23	39.4	18.4	21.0
Softball	20	25	16	34.3	20.3	14.0
Camping	22	24	21	37.7	19.2	18.5
Tennis	12	14	10	20.7	11.3	9.4
Racquetball	7	10	4	11.7	8.1	3.6
Calisthenics	15	17	13	25.6	13.7	11.9
Volleyball	15	17	14	25.8	13.4	12.4
Basketball	14	23	6	24.6	18.9	5.7
Hiking	20	22	18	33.9	17.7	16.2
Bicycling	31	29	33	52.6	23.2	29.4

Source: Gallup Opinion Polls, *Gallup Leisure Activities Index 1986* (Princeton: 1986), p. 11.

While 51% of American adults participate in some type of fitness program, Gallup's research reveals that 44% exercise on a daily basis—a statistic that has remained remarkably stable over the past decade. Table 4.2 highlights the trend in daily exercise over the past 25 years. In 1961, just prior to the fitness boom, only one American in four said they exercised daily. By 1977 that number had nearly doubled.

Table 4.2   25-Year Trend in Daily Exercise

Year	Engage in Daily Exercise
1985	44%
1982	47%
1980	46%
1977	47%
1961	24%

Source: Gallup Opinion Polls, *Gallup Leisure Activities Index 1986* (Princeton: 1986), p. 85.

As a group women are almost as likely as men to exercise on a daily basis—42% of the women in Gallup's survey said they exercised daily compared with 47% of the men. Another point of comparison is age—women's exercise habits are not substantially influenced by age. The Gallup findings reveal that women over age 30 are as likely to exercise daily as their younger counterparts. The same trend, however, does not hold true for men. Men over 30 are substantially less likely to exercise on a daily basis than are men under 30. Other demographic factors, such as income, education, and occupation, seem to have relatively little to do with whether people participate in a daily exercise program.

Gallup did find, however, notable regional differences in exercise habits, and these findings are presented in Table 4.3. For both men and women, those living in the West are substantially more likely to engage in daily exercise than people living in other regions of the country.

Table 4.3 Incidence of Daily Exercise by Region

Region	Total	Men	Women
East	44%	46%	41%
Midwest	41%	45%	39%
South	41%	41%	40%
West	55%	58%	51%

Source: Gallup Opinion Polls, *Gallup Leisure Activities Index 1986* (Princeton: 1986), p. 86.

What do these demographic factors imply for the health club industry? Although most demographic factors have little correlation with daily exercise programs, age and socioeconomic status are positively correlated with health club membership. Table 4.4 presents Gallup's demographic segmentations among health club members. About one in ten age-qualifying Americans belong to a fitness center, with membership slightly higher in the West (14%) and somewhat lower in the South (7%) than for the nation as a whole. For those adults under the age of 30, membership is almost twice as high as the national percentage.

Table 4.4 Health Club Membership Demographics

Total Adults	11%
Men	10%
Women	11%
Age	
Under 30 years	19%
18-24 years	18%
25-29 years	22%
30-49 years	12%
50 & older	3%
50-64 years	5%
65 & older	1%
Household Income	
$50,000 & over	23%
$40,000-$49,000	18%
$25,000-$39,000	10%
$15,000-$24,999	11%
$10,000-$14,999	6%
Under $10,000	4%
Education	
College graduates	17%
College incomplete	15%
High school grad.	10%
Less than HS grad.	2%
Occupation	
Profess. & business	16%
Clerical & sales	20%
Manual workers	8%
Non-labor force	8%
Young Urban Professionals	24%
Region	
East	12%
Midwest	11%
South	7%
West	14%

Source: Gallup Opinion Polls, *Gallup Leisure Activities Index 1986* (Princeton: 1986), p. 91.

The percentage of health club memberships is even higher among the upper-income population groups. For example, among individuals in the highest income categories—the young urban professionals categories—almost one in four (24%) belong to a health club. Given that income increases with age, the relative youth of health club members combined with their high income is very striking and presents numerous growth opportunities for the fitness industry. The developer entering the market must exploit these opportunities to his/her advantage.

As the aforementioned statistics attest, health clubs attract a disproportionate number of high-income, well-educated individuals. What is not so readily apparent, however, is that different club types—for example, the tennis club, the racquet club, and the multipurpose sport club—appeal to different customer segments, just as different sport activities appeal to different types of people. The various customer profiles suggest that different club types have different challenges and different requirements for success and growth in the fitness industry.

Tennis

Tennis remains the most popular of all racquet sports, yet recent research points to the fact that the popularity of tennis has waned in the past ten years. A.C. Nielsen's survey of sports participation in Table 4.5 shows a 21% decline in tennis between 1979 and 1982.

Table 4.6 presents Simmons' market data that corroborate the Nielsen finding with a more detailed breakdown of yearly tennis participation. A noteworthy point in evaluating the data is that though the number of tennis players decreased over the years, the degree of decline—as seen by the percent of change in projected players—is stabilizing.

Table 4.5 Tennis Participation Trends

	Proj. Indiv. Participants (000) 1982	% Change in Proj. Part. '82 vs. '79	Proj. Indiv. Participants (000) 1979	% Change in Proj. Part. '79 vs. '76	Proj. Indiv. Participants (000) 1976	% Change in Proj. Part. '76 vs. '73	Proj. Indiv. Participants (000) 1973
Tennis	25,450	−21%	32,271	+10%	29,201	+45%	20,158

Source: A.C. Nielsen Company Sports Participation Survey, 1982.

used their health club at least 5 days a week, while 24% had not used their club at all during the last month.[8] The club operator needs to develop some guidelines to estimate the extent of club usage. Since not all members will be active users, a health club is able to "oversell" its memberships. By overselling, the club not only brings in extra revenue but also ensures active usage. Members do not want an overcrowded club, nor do they want an empty club. They want to work out in a lively and inviting environment. The club operator must estimate that middle point.

There are no hard and fast rules to estimating club usage, but demographic composition of the market can provide some insights. Research findings imply that club usage will vary by the types of amenities offered, member exercise habits, and geographic location.

A club's facilities are used much more often than its services. For example, IRSA found that the top three amenities preferred by club members are weight machines, racquetball courts, and spa facilities. The most infrequently used amenities included services such as tournaments, racquet lessons/clinics, and game arrangement programs. The research findings imply that the infrequent use of services by club members is not necessarily because the services are unappealing, but may very well be due to clubs' passive management of such services.[9]

An individual's previous exercise history is also a good predictor of club usage. IRSA's research found that first time members use their health club the least and that frequency of usage increases with membership years. The most frequent users also tend to be those individuals that were active exercisers before joining their health club. As can be seen in Table 4.8—which presents the differences in club usage according to members' pre-joining activity level—71% of those who were active exercisers before joining, use their club 3+ times per week.[10]

Table 4.8   Club Usage According to Pre-joining Activity Levels

Pre-joining Activity	Percent Using Club 3+ Times/Wk First 3 Months of Membership	% Using Club 3+ Times/Wk Now
Inactive	55%	69%
On & Off Exercisers	57%	70%
Active Exercisers	71%	78%
On & Off Racquet	44%	67%
Active Racquet	56%	72%

Source: "Why People Join," An IRSA Special Report, 1986, p. 64.

Following along the same lines as Gallup's findings that health club membership is higher in the West, IRSA's research found that health club members in the West also use their clubs more often than members in other parts of the country.[11]

Market Analysis

A market analysis defines the state of the industry, the potential customers (demographic segments, their motivations, and their unmet needs), and the competition and environmental conditions (governmental regulation, for example) that may affect a business venture. After all relevant factors have been defined, the analysis is used strategically to identify viable alternatives and ultimately determine the best alternative.

A fitness facility market analysis can be divided into four steps:

1. Identification of demographic and regional/climate factors;
2. Determination of trade area;
3. Evaluation of demand potential within the trade area; and
4. Evaluation of supply within the trade area.

The market analysis must narrowly focus on specific community data, since even within a region consumer demand varies from one community to another, depending on factors such as income, recreational attitudes, age, climate, and interest in other sports.

Thus far, this chapter has identified demographic and regional/climate factors that impact the fitness market. The health club developer, manager, or analyst must apply these variables in further analyzing specific market areas.

The next step is to identify the club's trade area. A trade area is defined by the geographic distance individuals are willing to travel to reach their health club. Table 3.1 and the discussion in Chapter 3 gives a general account of the distances people are willing to drive to reach their clubs. The average driving time is estimated at 10 to 15 minutes or approximately a 5 to 7 mile radius.

A well-defined trade area gives the club's market analysis a focus and a base point for the strategic planning process. Marketing tactics can then be applied and adjusted to execute the strategies.

Market analysis, however, is not simply laying a template of demographic factors and club features over the market to define a trade area. Individuals' perceptions greatly influence the distances they are willing to travel. Trade area is actually a "trade-off area," for although most people will go to the facility that is most conveniently located for them, they may be willing to travel longer distances for more attractive club features. Therefore, the image people hold of a club is a key factor in determining trade area and evaluating demand potential.

Health club trade areas can be defined according to three types of perceived business categories—is the health club perceived as a convenience business, a shopping business, or a specialty business? Most health clubs are perceived as either convenience or shopping businesses.[12]

A club that is perceived as a convenience business has the smallest trade area of the three business categories. Such clubs offer a minimum amount of services and engage in minimal selling efforts. The consumer often purchases a convenience club membership as an impulse item and is generally not willing to travel more than eight to ten minutes to reach the club.[13]

A shopping business commands a moderate trade area since an individual is generally willing to travel a maximum of 16 minutes to reach a shopping club. Competition between shopping clubs is often based on much more than just price. If a club's offerings are perceived as being available at different locations, price becomes an important factor. If, however, the club is perceived as being different, quality and style become the determining factors and price is less important.[14]

The specialty club commands the largest trade area because the club is perceived as offering something unique (it may be a product, service, setting, or reputation). When purchasing a specialty club membership, price and distance are not considerations. Members are willing to spend extra money and travel well over 16 minutes to attend the club.[15]

In some market areas, a tennis club may function as a specialty club if other tennis-playing options are extremely limited. A classic example in the specialty fitness category is the health spa resort. Many well-known spas attract guests from a nationwide market.

A valuable analytical technique for evaluating a trade area, and its potential, is to define the trade area from the club's point of view and then compare that definition to the actual trade area as defined by the geographic location of the club's membership. If the two definitions are substantially different, the club has an image problem. Marketing tactics can be employed to realign the club's image and its defined trade area. For example, if the objective is to attract people from a larger trade area, then the club needs to cultivate the image of a shopping good or specialty good. Long-term customer satisfaction and repeat business must be developed. This goal is both time and capital intensive; it may require the club to invest in high quality facilities and new features and to hire a service-conscious staff and a "name" pro.[16]

The final component of a fitness facility market analysis is an evaluation of market supply. This task requires a survey within the defined target area of existing and proposed facilities and the amenities that will be offered. Independent research must be performed to determine the level of demand in any specific location and the supply of facilities responding to that demand. In addition, the developer must identify the strengths and weaknesses of each competing facility in an effort to define which customer needs are being met and which are not; this will, in turn, provide a "road map" of potential market niches that could be filled with a new club.

Even if an area appears to be saturated in sheer number of clubs, it does not necessarily mean that the demand is being satisfied. Clubs can be unsuccessful because of poor management and unprofitable pricing schedules. They may also suffer from physical factors such as wind, obnoxious noises, odors, or other unpleasant influences emanating from adjacent industrial or institutional uses. Poor construction features such as outdoor tennis courts that face east and west (where players must face the sun) or weight rooms that are too small and lack adequate ventilation may repel potential members. Clubs may be unsuccessful because of bad location; people are becoming unwilling to travel to and through neighborhoods with high crime levels. All of these factors should be classified by the developer as club weaknesses.

Attention must also be given to public and quasi-public facilities. Municipalities have been expanding the number of public recreation amenities they offer, and they have also been improving on the quality of their facilities. In addition, facilities at schools and colleges are often available to the general public when not being used by students during school hours. Such nonschool playing time coincides with prime time—immediately after working hours—at private clubs.

Resort and residential complexes that satisfy the needs of potential club members also represent competition. Resort hotels often offer attractively low membership fees or hourly rates to permanent residents in the surrounding community to offset the fixed operating expenses at their facilities and to increase club occupancy percentages. In the sunbelt states, there is scarcely a suburban condominium or rental complex of more than 100 units being constructed without tennis facilities, pools, and weight rooms. Such complexes fulfill the requirements of all but the most diehard athletic-prone residents and may severely cut into the market for a new private club.

Finally, the analysis of market supply would not be complete without considering the number of new facilities planned for the area, as well as new amenities that are to be added at existing clubs. Such facilities could be completely new public or private ventures. They could also represent expansion programs at existing facilities.

This final segment of the competitive analysis is often overlooked, and the outcome can be devastating for the club developer when halfway through construction an identical facility opens in the same market area. Therefore, local planning or building permit departments should be consulted, and the total number of existing and projected clubs in the target market must be analyzed. If the developer finds him/herself in the position of having started development action when it is learned that a competitive facility is planned for a nearby site, it is critical to be the first to open for business. Being first to open gives the club a first-mover advantage—an important success factor since it can help protect a club from the eroding effects of new competition.

Operations
Management

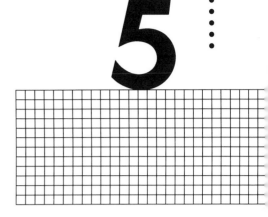

Health clubs, like any other business, are intent on staying in business. This objective is particularly challenging given the volatility of the health club industry. Fads clearly dominate the fitness market. Many clubs are opened to ride the newest exercise wave to success; their doors are closed only a few years later when the tide changes. Clubs close for a variety of reasons, including the competitive environment, underpricing of services, overbuilding of facilities, and poor management.

This does not necessarily imply that fitness clubs are not good business ventures. On the contrary, many health clubs are very profitable. IRSA's 1987 survey of member clubs found that net operating profits ranged, on average, from $150,000 to $550,000 depending upon the type of fitness club and the amenities offered. The most successful clubs in the survey had a net operating profit range of $225,000 to $800,000. Again, the range of operating profits depended upon the type of amenities the club offered; tennis clubs generally had the lowest operating profits and multipurpose sport clubs reported the highest profit levels.[1] Table 5.1 presents a complete breakdown of operating profit by club type.

Table 5.1 Operating Profit by Club Type

	Average Clubs		Most Successful Clubs	
Club Type	Net Oper. Profit	Ratio to Total Rev.	Net Oper. Profit	Ratio to Total Rev.
Tennis	$156,262	25.6%	$227,814	42.0%
Racquetball/Squash	189,571	30.8%	290,443	47.7%
Fitness	201,002	31.3%	649,867	48.7%
Multirecreation	337,415	29.6%	N/A	N/A
Multirecreation with Outdoor Pool	530,036	30.9%	800,359	49.2%

Note: Club types are defined as follows:

Tennis Clubs: clubs with indoor and/or outdoor tennis courts; no other courts of any type; no indoor pool; no staffed fitness center.

Racquetball and/or Squash Clubs: clubs with racquetball and/or squash courts; no other courts of any type; no indoor pool; no staffed fitness center.

Fitness Clubs: clubs with weight machines, weights, fitness equipment, and/or dance and exercise classes; no courts, may have an indoor pool.

Multirecreation Clubs: clubs with one type of court and a staffed fitness center; or clubs with more than one type of court with or without a staffed fitness center.

Multirecreation Clubs with Indoor Pools: same as multirecreation but with an indoor pool.

Source: IRSA, "Profiles of Success—1987 State of the Industry Report," 1987, pp. 22-23.

The survey results indicate that long-term profits were achieved through expense control. The more successful clubs actually grossed less revenue than the average clubs, yet they realized higher net operating profits by controlling expenses, particularly their payroll expense. Payroll expense for the more successful clubs was 6.5% to 11% less than payroll expense for the average club.[2]

In addition to expense control, performance ratios can be used to help evaluate club profitability. There are ten key ratios used to judge a club's health:[3]

1. Revenue per membership—total revenues at end of fiscal year divided by total number of memberships at end of fiscal year;

2. Revenue per square foot—total revenues at end of fiscal year divided by total indoor square footage (including any areas covered by air structures for all or part of the year);

3. Percent dues of total revenues—the sum of membership dues plus initiation fees at the end of the fiscal year divided by total revenues obtained during the same period;

4. Increase (decrease) in revenues—total revenues of previous fiscal year subtracted from total revenues of current fiscal year

and divided by the previous fiscal year's revenues: for example, to calculate the increase from 1984 to 1985, subtract 1984 revenues from 1985 revenues and divide the result by 1984 revenues;

5. Return on sales—pretax profit for fiscal year divided by total revenues for fiscal year;

6. Return on equity—pretax profit divided by the sum of capital stock plus capital surplus plus retained earnings;

7. Operating expense—the sum of direct and indirect expenses divided by total revenues for fiscal year;

8. Membership growth—total number of memberships from previous fiscal year subtracted from total number of memberships for current fiscal year and that figure divided by the previous year's total;

9. Membership attrition—total number of dropped memberships divided by total number of memberships at the beginning of the same fiscal year; and

10. Weekly usages per member—the total number of memberships at the beginning of the fiscal year added to the total number at the end of the same fiscal year. Divide this figure by two to obtain (A). Divide the total number of visits by all members to the club during the fiscal year by (A) to obtain (B). Divide (B) by 52.

Management

Good management is the most crucial variable in the equation for a successful health club. The successful health club requires management that not only goes with the flow of the industry but also works to anticipate the direction of the flow. It needs a management that can work in tandem with industry trends and guide its club members through its ups and downs. Management must also be able to assess industry opportunities and take the initiative to exploit those opportunities to its advantage.

Basically, three kinds of people operate health clubs. Each has characteristics that are essential to running a successful club, but one skill is not sufficient by itself.

The first kind of manager is the sport aficionado. All the sports industries—for example, golf, bowling, and skiing—tend to attract such people—people who bring with them enthusiasm for and technical skill in an activity. Unfortunately, these attributes alone are not enough to make an athletic facility profitable. A health club requires capital investments, and the need to generate cash to meet ever-increasing operational expenses is seldom filled by the professional athlete.

The second kind, the professional operator, is also attracted to health clubs. Without skills that are critical to the enterprise, including marketing, accounting, and sales abilities, the professional operator, however, can only follow instructions and collect a paycheck. Without constant direction or training by the owner, there is a high risk of poor service in the club and inefficiently operated business.

Unlike the above two types of managers, the investor-manager is concerned with cash flow and profitability rather than playing or membership concerns. However, the mere concentration on costs, without a sensitivity for the needs of any services to members, is not likely to produce a successful operation.

To manage a profit-making health club, abilities in planning, supervising, and controlling are necessary. Managers must be able to project a course of action to which available resources will be committed; they must have skills to direct each employee in the facility to fulfill specific job functions; and they must know how to conserve resources in order to perpetuate the operation. In all these activities, appreciation of the club's activities is assumed, but planning, supervising, and controlling are the areas of expertise that are necessary for a successful facility.

The challenges to club managers are both external and internal. The external challenge is to capture the market of prospective members by taking advantage of the public's increasing awareness of and interest in fitness. The most crucial task to achieving this goal is marketing.

Marketing

A club manager can take several steps to properly market a project.[4] The first step is to assess the club's strengths. Once these strengths are known, the features that are rated as the most attractive to prospective members should be made the focus of the marketing plan.

The club's strengths should also be compared with its competition to determine the club's unique selling proposition: What makes this club stand apart from its competitors? This unique selling point defines the "position" the club holds in the marketplace. A marketable position is essential to an effective marketing plan. If a unique position cannot be discerned, the club will have to do something—change or add a feature—to create a unique position.

After the marketable aspects of the club are determined, the club's image must be defined. Image is the perception the public holds of a club, and it is closely related to the club's market position. Image can be defined in terms of the club's size, its social life, or the personality of its staff. Obviously, it is much easier to sell a positive image than to create a new image.

The importance of a good staff in attracting and retaining new members should not be overlooked. A good staff is a marketing advantage that is easily exploited. Qualified and enthusiastic teaching pros, fitness counselors, and aerobics instructors are keys to keeping a club's membership happy and to encouraging new members to join. To use a staff to its fullest, the club manager should be sure that every staff member is aware of the club's current marketing program. The staff should also be encouraged to actively support recruitment efforts through an incentive program.

The location of a club is another asset that many managers ignore when developing their marketing plans. Location can easily be played up in promotional messages to attract members. For example, a club located in an industrial park would place marketing emphasis on before work, after work, and noontime programs. Downtown clubs should cater not only to the work crowd but also to the shoppers who come downtown to shop once or twice a week.

Price is another easy way to capture a marketplace, but it can be a dangerous tool. There is always the possibility that a new club will open with lower prices. A price war can develop, and often both clubs come out losers.

Once members are attracted to a club, the club's programs have to do the job of keeping those members loyal to the club. Two program methods can be used to stake out market position. One method is to offer more programs than the competition; the other method is to excel in one area. It is up to the manager to assess accurately the club's strengths and weaknesses and determine the appropriate program method.

Convenience is a sales tool that is related to location but emphasizes services offered to members. For example, opening club doors at 5:00

a.m. is a convenience that caters to the early-rising executive; childcare facilities are conveniences that target mothers. As a general rule, conveniences are not to be used to develop marketing positions that attract new members. Rather, they are simply support programs to an already established marketing position.[5]

A club's current membership roster provides a wealth of information to the club manager who is assessing demographic composition for the marketing campaign. By reviewing the membership roster as to who uses the club, the manager can "guestimate" the demographic profile of the target audience. Club members are often categorized into several segments: single males, single females, married couples, families, housewives, former athletes, older businessmen, senior citizens, young adults, and so forth. Determining what features are most attractive to each segment provides direction when targeting new members and developing marketing programs.

Managers must use creative programming to increase the number of club members in the present market and to encourage current members to use the club and its profit centers more frequently. Sophisticated operators are presently trying to tap the 50- to 60-year-old market that until recently was not well represented in club membership. This group of people is generally affluent and has time to participate but in the past was not often seen as a potential member segment. Today the interest in fitness exists in all age groups, and senior citizens are interested in the club that offers programs to address their specific needs.

Another lucrative segment to tap is the youth market. Encouraging membership among young adults builds club loyalty at an early age and expands the club's membership foundation. The club has a good opportunity to upgrade the youth memberships to adult memberships. Other operators are promoting use of club facilities to traveling business people and vacationers. Such attempts to develop virgin markets are always in addition to efforts to expand the existing market. Club ladders, tournaments, and social functions are important elements of money-making facilities with which the manager must also be concerned.

Current members are a great marketing resource for a club. For example, members bring in guests and thereby introduce potential members to the club. Members also provide word-of-mouth advertising when they discuss their workout activities with friends and generate additional revenue when they shop in the pro shop or utilize other club profit centers.

It is not enough for the manager simply to know whom to target and which messages should be emphasized in the marketing campaign. The messages must reach the target, and this requires effective advertising. As a first step in evaluating media alternatives, the manager should look at where the competition advertises. Most likely, the competition's trials and errors have found the most effective media vehicles. Direct mail, though expensive, can be a very effective vehicle to reach the target audience residing within a five-mile radius from the club. Of course, once an effective vehicle is determined, the message must be appropriate and presented in a clear and interesting fashion; a catchy slogan or a jingle often enhances the advertising message.

A health club is in the people business, and its concerns for people should not stop with its members but should extend to all community members. A final component to a marketing campaign, therefore, should include public relations. Good community relations gives a marketing campaign a capitalization factor and gives advertising an edge that money can't buy. Donating the use of a club's facilities, for example, to a charity organization may not sell additional memberships, but it does enhance the image the club holds in the public's eye. It also instills a sense of pride in the club's staff that, in turn, makes that staff proud to sell additional memberships.

Marketing is the primary external challenge facing today's club manager. However, internal concerns are just as important—all the money and energy invested in marketing will not sell the club if the manager does not have a quality club to sell. Therefore, attention must be paid to the most mundane internal issues, such as the day-to-day operating details of traffic controls, maintenance, equipment upkeep, sanitary cleanliness, and operating hours. There are also internal concerns that have a much more long-term and structural impact on the club. These issues include staffing considerations, pricing, membership structure, insurance, and state codes and regulations.

Staffing Considerations

One of the most important assets of any business is its employees and this factor is especially critical to the success of fitness facilities. A fitness workout is a highly personal experience of the club member: physically it impacts on the member's health and body; mentally it impacts on the member's self-image and ego. As a result, a service-oriented operating philosophy and staff are requirements for successful recreational projects.

Although there are no general rules of thumb guiding an appropriate staff to member ratio mix, it is often assumed that the larger the staff the greater the member service. A staff to member ratio, however, can be deceptive and should not be taken at face value as an indicator of a club's servicing capabilities. For example, a club with a high proportion of sales personnel, relative to fitness personnel, may have a very good total staff to member ratio but in reality the club would rank very low on member service. The sales personnel sell memberships. It is the fitness personnel who guide and teach members how to use the facility and its equipment.

The number of personnel staffing a facility will vary by club type and amenities offered. The most luxurious health spas and spa clubs maintain service-oriented staff to member ratios of up to four to one. These types of clubs are targeting the consumer that is shopping for personal pampering. At the other extreme, some clubs target the independent exerciser whose primary concern is having a place to work out and who is not interested in personal attention. These types of club may only staff personnel to handle administrative functions and maintenance duties. In between these two extremes are the clubs offering a range of personnel and member service.

Managers and their assistants are responsible for coordinating the efforts of all the administrative, fitness, and auxiliary personnel the club employs. The hours the club is open will directly affect the number of employees the manager needs. The manager must translate job functions into monthly and daily work schedules for personnel in marketing (development of new participants, membership renewals, newsletters, and special events), maintenance (courts, equipment, locker rooms, and public areas), and accounting (invoicing, accounts receivable, accounts payable, and reports).

Although the importance of athletic expertise should not be diminished, a good club manager must have a background that is more business oriented than exercise oriented. A good club manager is also able to give sufficient and undivided attention to the concerns of all employee segments. The manager who only attends to administrative affairs loses touch with the club and its members. The manager who spends too much time in his or her office, receiving and reading reports, is unaware of problems like crowding and poor maintenance. The manager who spends too much time in the field is a manager-in-absence, and the club is left to operate in its own haphazard way.

The manager sets the tone for the entire club, even in a chain operation; and the quality of the facility is a reflection of the manager's expertise and commitment.

In addition to management, the administrative staff is composed of salespeople and clerical/support workers. As the competitive nature of the fitness industry grows more intense, clubs are realizing the importance of active membership growth. Therefore, more and more clubs are referring to their salespeople as membership directors or coordinators since the term salesperson tends to carry a negative connotation in many people's minds.[6]

Some clubs, in order to get more mileage out of their personnel investment, will have administrative personnel double as fitness instructors, or vice versa. Such an arrangement may make economical sense, but it detracts from member service. How available will that fitness instructor be to members if the instructor needs to increase sales efforts?

The fitness personnel are the most important employee segment in the service-oriented club. These are the people who profile, program, and instruct club members. The extent of a club's fitness staff will vary by club and amenities offered.

The fitness director heads the fitness staff and is responsible for seeing that class instructors and other staff deliver a consistent level of service. Unlike the club manager, a good fitness director has a background that is more exercise than business oriented.

Profiling personnel take the member's health profile: pulse rate, target heart range, weight, and measurements. Staff performing these tasks can be laymen with some training. More complicated profiling, however, requires medically trained personnel. A knowledgeable profiling staff will have degrees in exercise physiology or have certifications from creditable institutes, such as American College of Sports Medicine (ACSM) or the Institute of Aerobics Research (founded by Dr. Kenneth Cooper).[7]

Instructors hold one of the most important staff positions in the health club facility. Club members have daily contact with their instructors, and it is the instructor who affects the member the most with guidance and teachings. Depending upon the amenities offered, the health club may be staffed with exercise and aerobic instructors, weight training instructors, and racquet sports instructors.

Certification of instructors is a growing controversy in the fitness industry, especially as more and more people report serious injuries because of their exercise programs and the instructions they receive. No laws require instructor certification, but exercise associations and institutes, in response to the growing number of injury complaints, are establishing voluntary requirements. Both the ACSM and the Institute for Aerobic Research award certification degrees to aerobic fitness instructors successfully completing their respective training programs. Many weight equipment manufacturers, such as Nautilus, provide training for weight equipment instructors. Clubs may also establish their own in-house training programs.[8]

Racquet sports instructors do not need university training and/or certification to teach racquet sports, but a club that has a teaching professional on staff has a valuable resource. A teaching pro is a recognizable figure to a club's members and potential members, and this recognition can be very valuable when incorporated into a marketing campaign. For example, a pro projects quality, and this enhances a club's image. The club can extend that image by establishing the pro as the club's media spokesperson.

Staffing a club with good employees is a stiff challenge; keeping those employees is an even greater challenge. The more successful clubs recognize that an hourly or monthly salary is only one form of employee compensation, and it is often one of the least effective employee motivators. Compensation systems, with either financial or nonfinancial rewards, play an important role in motivating employees to do a good job once they are hired. For example, public praise, daily manager/staff interaction, and unexpected rewards for performing extra member services motivate the staff to work hard and to promote the club. Generous compensation programs instill club loyalty in the staff. Although IRSA's research is not able to draw a clear causal relationship, it does appear that the clubs that recognize employee compensation beyond a base salary also enjoy low member attrition rates.[9]

Pricing and Membership Structure

In light of the fitness industry's volatility and competitive wars, membership growth and retention are dominant manager concerns. One of the biggest member retention problems may be how to increase prices without alienating current members. The key is to instill the concept of perceived value—if prices need to be raised, members must feel they are getting more value for their dollar. Clearly, a club's pricing structure is critical to attracting and retaining members. It is also critical to a club's cash flow structure and overall profitability.

In the interest of making prices attractive to as many people as possible, fitness facilities have developed an array of price plans. In most cases the membership plans satisfy both the customer's need for an affordable membership and the club's need for profitable margins. In other cases, however, a club makes the mistake of overextending its customer offers; as a result, many clubs end up closing their doors.

Lifetime memberships used to be the staple offering in the fitness industry. In recent years, however, many states have outlawed these contracts since they are not in the consumers' best interest. The agreement favors the club since most members move, die, or lose interest in the club before they get a fair return on the investment. The more reputable clubs that still sell lifetime memberships also offer options to make the arrangement more equitable: a member can freeze the membership if going away for a substantial period of time, a member has the option to transfer (sell) his/her membership, and/or a fair refund is available if the member becomes physically unable to make use of the health club.[10]

As competition for members becomes more fierce, more health clubs are offering memberships on a short-term basis—for example, one-month or three-month trial memberships. These offerings are designed to induce the consumer to try a club membership; the idea is that after trying the membership the customer will be satisfied enough to join as a permanent member.

The initiation fee plus monthly dues is becoming the more common type of membership structure. The reason for its appeal is that it has been found to be a profitable structure for the club and an affordable arrangement for the consumer. The initiation fee is a one-time nonrefundable charge, and, depending upon the type of club, the charge may be quite substantial. For the consumer, monthly dues spread the membership costs out over a year's time; for the club, the monthly dues guarantee a regular in-coming cash flow and lessen "renewal decisions" that may contribute to member attrition.

This book does not provide industry averages for membership fees because dues and initiation costs vary considerably. The most important factors that influence membership fees are the facility's quality and its competitive position in the market. For reference, Table 5.2 lists some of the most expensive clubs in the United States today. These annual fees are for a single adult membership but do not include initiation fees.

Table 5.2   Annual Membership Fees of Selected Health Clubs

Club Name	City	Annual Fee
Excelsior Club	New York	$1,500
Executive Fitness	New York	$1,400
Vertical Club	New York	$ 720
The Sports Club	Los Angeles	$1,500
The Sporting Club	Atlanta	$1,260
The Veranda Club	Dallas	$1,200
The Bay Club	San Francisco	$ 960
The East Bank Club	Chicago	$ 900
Boston Athletic Club	Boston	$ 840
Capitol Hill Squash & Nautilus Club	Washington D.C.	$ 660

Source: Jennifer Seabury, "The Price of Staying Fit," *City Sports* (San Francisco Edition, February, 1988) p. 47.

Two other fee structures that are commonly used are the fixed price and the a la carte plans. These options may actually have been started by racquet clubs where members frequently have the choice between "unlimited use" or "pay-as-you-play" options. The fixed price plan allows members to participate in every amenity, system, and service for a flat fee. The a la carte plan allows members to join at a low rate and then purchase additional services if they choose to participate in additional activities. Clubs will often offer multilevel membership plans that include both the fixed price and the a la carte options. Higher levels of membership, at higher prices, include a wider range of services. Sometimes there are wholly separate and substantially more luxurious locker rooms and spa facilities provided for members who opt for the higher price plan. The lower level plan is a no-frills option. The membership provides use of basic equipment with Spartan spa facilities and a few amenities.[11]

Importance of Insurance

One aspect of operations which a manager must consider is proper insurance. Although insurance expenses may seem excessive, the costs associated with a major fire, burglary, vandalism, or a liability lawsuit could debilitate a club.

Property insurance should include coverage for the real property, personal property, and optional business interruption. Coverage of these three components depends on their respective values. For real and personal properties, insurance companies rely upon replacement costs. Real property coverage encompasses the replacement cost of the building only, exclusive of the land and foundation. This value should be based on an appraisal. Personal property refers to the furniture, fixtures, and equipment. The value of these items usually is determined by taking inventory of the building contents and assigning a value to each item. Business interruption insurance pays a portion of fixed cash flows during periods when the club is closed for reconstruction following an incident covered by the policy. Fixed expenses to be considered for estimating business interruption coverage include rent, mortgage payments, minimum utility costs, and salaries for nondispensable employees.

Insurance for real and personal property should cover at least 80% of value. Business interruption coverage should pay at least 50% of fixed operating expenses.

Another critically important area of coverage for a club is liability insurance. As the result of injuries and accidents, clubs are facing personal injury lawsuits from members. Of course, clubs should take preventive actions to reduce the likelihood of these suits, such as providing proper instruction, issuing appropriate warnings, and evaluating the capabilities of members before allowing them to proceed. Nonetheless, should a suit arise, a club must have liability insurance to prevent potential catastrophic losses.

As an operation management issue and an appraisal question, major liability losses are avoidable through proper insurance coverage. Rates usually are based upon gross revenues, although some insurance companies set rates based on interior floor areas. One source quoted a rate of $2.55 per $100 of gross annual receipts for a $1,000,000 comprehensive liability policy. Liability coverage under this policy included general club operations, product liability, personal injury, and invasions of privacy.[12] Even if a club does not have liability insurance, an appraiser should make an adequate allowance for insurance expenses in the Income Approach.

Government Regulation

Consumer interest in fitness is strong and many health clubs are thriving, but a good many clubs are also failing. Some clubs fail because of legitimate reasons—such as undercapitalization or poor management; other clubs fail for illegitimate reasons—fraudulent and deceptive business practices.

Potential health club members complain of high-pressure sales tactics and false advertising. More than 3,000 complaints had been filed with the Federal Trade Commission (FTC) by 1985,[13] yet, because the clubs are hard to police because they are so numerous and so easy to open. Intent to commit fraud must be proven in court, and intent is notoriously hard to establish. Prosecution for abuse, therefore, is often difficult and regulation has been largely ineffectual. As a result, sudden club closings leave many members stranded—their investments simply washed away.[14]

A major source of trouble for many health clubs begins with their financing.[15] Most clubs, especially the storefront clubs and the multipurpose sports clubs that do not have major structural investments like swimming pools and tennis courts, require little capital because the equipment and real estate are often leased. Club operators rely mainly on fees from new members for their cash flow. Some clubs, with proper management, succeed within their limitations; but other clubs resort to deceptive practices to turn a profit. For example, clubs have been known to continue selling memberships even when creditors are foreclosing on defaulted loans.[16]

The stringent financing conditions also create intense pressure on sales people that sometimes gets turned onto potential members. Some clubs have been charged with using coercion, intimidation, or severe embarrassment to get people to take out club memberships. The club allegedly tricked people into signing binding membership contracts and then used collection agencies to collect the fees.[17]

A contract by itself does not make a club guilty of deceptive and illegitimate business practices. A great many legitimate clubs require customer contracts. The key difference between a good club requiring a contract and a bad club requiring a contract lies in what the contract says or does not say. Hard sell clubs tend to use extreme contracts, written in confusing terms and in small print. The contracts usually do not offer any extra information, such as references to the state laws that govern customer refunds. A well-intentioned contract, on the other hand, includes reference information as well as information specifying the club's facilities and services. This type of contract gives the club member the right to cancel the contract if the club substantially changes its facilities. In addition, a legitimate contract breaks out the initiation fee and monthly dues so a customer can see exactly how much must be paid and how much of a refund is permitted.[18]

Clubs that have lifetime membership fee structures rely on new sales for most of their revenues. As a result, these clubs put most of their energy into garnering new memberships rather than channeling their efforts into servicing existing members. A proposed revision to California's health studios law found that contract-based health club facilities generally invest 31% of their total revenues in attracting new sales.[19] Contract clubs do not necessarily use high pressure sales tactics or tricky membership agreements, but they are more prone to those problems than are clubs that have a monthly dues structure.

Clubs that use a monthly dues payment plan are depending more on renewals than on new memberships for their revenues. The monthly dues structure initiates more of a member service focus because the clubs want to encourage members to renew their memberships.

Most of the legislation that has been passed by states in the past few years has been directed at the problems caused by contract-based clubs. In 1985, however, the FTC decided against issuing federal rules for health clubs. The commission did not find the abusive practices pervasive enough to warrant federal legislation. Instead, the commission felt that any misconduct would best be handled through case-by-case enforcement. In their finding, the commission asserted that regulation would make the health club industry less attractive to investors.[20]

At the state level, however, action has been taken. In 1983 17 states had health club laws; by 1987 27 states had instituted health club laws. Connecticut instituted a registration fee that is collected from clubs, and the money is used to reimburse victims in fraud cases. Maryland now has a health spa commissioner to enforce state regulations. Most of the state laws have concentrated on bonding requirements—clubs are required to post bonds to cover potential losses that consumers may incur.[21]

In addition to state regulation for consumer protection, the health club operator needs to be aware of and adhere to state and local health board requirements. Health boards focus on issues that are physically and structurally oriented. For example, health boards may set temperature limits for a club's spa facilities. Many state health departments have requirements regarding the actual physical layout of a health club, for example, requiring clubs with swimming pools to locate their shower and toilet the facilities adjacent to swimming pools.[22]

The political and legislative environment affects the success of any business venture and the health club industry is no exception. In fact, with the controversies brewing over fraudulent business practices, injury complaints, and the need for accreditation, today's health club developer and operator must be all the more cognizant of regulations governing the operation of health club facilities.

The fitness industry is profitable but it is not a get-rich-quick type of business, although some club operators try to make it so. Proper management is the key to running a legitimate and profitable health club venture. Generally, an evaluation of the management's administrative and marketing skills is not within the scope of an appraiser's assignment. However, since many health club operations lease their real estate, appraisals may actually be business valuations.

In addition, from the mortgage lender's point of view, the risk in making a loan for a new facility is increasing, partially because of greater investment requirements in today's facilities than in the past. Consumer trends indicate that club members and potential members want to see diverse activities available in their health clubs.

The competitiveness in the health club industry has changed the ground rules, and the successes of a new project may very well turn on the degree of professionalism in management. Club managers need to start running their clubs like businesses. They need to think in terms of member service, strategic and feasible marketing plans, and profitability ratios. For these reasons, appraisers and lending institutions must closely scrutinize not only the facts and figures advancing the view that a given area will support another club but also the owner's will and ability to create a successful enterprise.

Financing

6

The general perception of the fitness industry among lenders is negative. The growth in demand for fitness facilities should, theoretically, create excellent opportunities for profitable operations; it logically should follow that lending money to these operations also should result in favorable returns to lending institutions. In reality, the competition for the health club member's dollar has been keen. In addition, poor management has resulted in consumer complaints against clubs and numerous club bankruptcies, closings, and foreclosures. As a result, financial institutions are not favorably disposed toward lending for recreational clubs.

Although many of these perceptions are true, profitable operations are identifiable through sound lending practices. This chapter discusses some of the facts regarding these adverse generalizations of the industry. Some guidelines are outlined that can help to indicate potentially delinquent operations. Current lending procedures for the fitness industry are presented, and ways to improve these practices are explored.

Fitness Industry Problems

An initial source of concern about health clubs comes from consumer complaints. These range from reports of misleading advertising and broken exercise machines to reports of clubs that move to another location or close entirely. The latter case becomes particularly troubling to consumers when they have paid a long-term, or even a lifetime, membership fee. Consumer frustrations are vented on numerous government agencies ranging from city hall to the state attorney general and Better Business Bureau.

Prospective lenders to health clubs should be wary of certain signals indicating that an enterprise's financial success could be endangered down the road. Successful health clubs are legitimate services that can be sold on their own merits without high pressure sales tactics. Member contracts are a good source to determine if the club can change services or hours, which probably would result in member dissatisfaction. Some clubs offer "special" deals to first-time club visitors that are often available later. Such sales gimmicks are not indicative of a long-term profitable enterprise that values favorable community relations.

Another adverse signal is on-going membership dues that are unusually low. These low rates generally do not generate sufficient income to cover expenses. Some clubs try to make up for this shortfall by selling more memberships with high initiation fees. While some turnover and attrition may be anticipated, a club relying heavily on initiation fees as an on-going revenue source will be in trouble soon after membership reaches capacity. A positive correlation to this axiom is that successful clubs should have good membership retention. As a rule of thumb, annual membership turnover rates below 30% indicate a well managed club, and membership turnover rates below 25% usually yield outstanding results.[1]

The capacity issue is another item lenders should investigate. Visit the club during noontime and between 6:00 p.m. and 8:00 p.m. to determine how peak flows are handled. Is additional membership limited by parking availability? number of lockers? unreasonable waits for the use of resistance machines? capacities of aerobics classes? It is reasonable to expect new members to follow the usage patterns of existing members, and tolerance of inconvenience usually is low if other options are available.

Other criteria worth investigating include the training of instructors and the maintenance and cleanliness of the facility. Asking instructors about their credentials is legitimate. Qualifications to consider include training in physical fitness, emergency first aid, cardiopulmonary resuscitation (CPR), and aerobic dance.

Lending Practices

Institutional financing for health and fitness club facilities is difficult to discuss with precise certainty because available data are limited and standardization is virtually nonexistent. Although fitness clubs in one form or another have been around for at least 30 years, their track record in the lending industry is not well documented. Lending practices seem to be based upon the experience of the individual lender rather than the collective experience of the industry.

The authors have attempted to broaden the information available to the industry through the publication of this book. One of our efforts was to survey 321 members of the Mortgage Bankers Association of America. The participants selected represent major lending institutions located in metropolitan areas throughout the United States. The response rate to the survey was 23.4%, which is considered good for a study of this type. The geographic distribution of the respondents is summarized in Table 6.1.

Table 6.1   Location in the United States of Respondent Lenders

Location	Number	Percent
Midwest	17	22.7
Southeast	13	17.3
Northeast	13	17.3
West	12	16.0
Southwest	9	12.0
National	11	14.7
Total	75	100.0

The survey included a full spectrum of lending institutions. Respondents represented mortgage bankers (36.5%), commercial banks (35.1%), savings and loans/savings banks (23.0%), and insurance companies (5.4%). The median size of the survey's typical lender had assets between $500 million and $2.5 million (42.9%). About 32.9% had assets over $2.5 billion, and 24.3% had assets under $500 million.

One of the most dramatic findings of the survey was that only 22% of lenders had financed "health/fitness/recreation projects." This percentage demonstrates the reluctance of lenders to finance these types of facilities and the industry's relative inexperience in this field. Of those that had financed these facilities, almost 86% of the lenders had financed between 1 and 5 recreational projects, 14% had financed 6 to 10 projects, and none had financed more than 10 projects.

Of those lenders who had financed fitness projects, 73% had financed multisport athletic clubs. This facility was by far the most popular type of club that lenders had financed. Other facilities financed were racquetball clubs (40%), tennis clubs (33%), storefront fitness clubs (27%), and health spas (7%). Most lenders had made either one or two loans for a given facility type, except for tennis clubs where the average number of loans per lender was three.

Mortgage Terms

Mortgage terms that lenders offer for fitness projects vary greatly. In our survey loan-to-value ratios, interest rates, debt-coverage ratios, financing fees, and loan terms all demonstrated little consistency. Our survey also confirmed the generally conservative attitude of lenders toward fitness facilities. These findings are summarized in a series of tables.

Our survey found that loan-to-value ratios for fitness facilities were slightly lower than for other commercial properties. The results indicated a median loan-to-value ratio of about 70%, which is below the typical range of 75% to 80%. One explanation could be that 82% of the respondents based their loans on the stabilized value of proposed developments rather than the discounted value as of completion of construction. A few respondents used alternative methods for determining loan amounts, including the income approach to value for an alternative commercial use and debt coverage ratios greater than 1.3 or 1.35. The low loan-to-value ratios and the alternative methods both point to conservative lending practices for fitness facilities.

Table 6.2   Typical Loan-to-Value Ratios

Loan/Value Ratio	Number of Respondents	Percent
80% or more	1	6.7
75%-79%	1	6.7
70%-74%	8	53.3
65%-69%	4	26.7
60%-64%	1	6.7
Under 60%	0	0
Total	15	100

Interest rates for fitness facilities were comparable to those of other investment properties. Almost 70% of the lenders quoted a typical interest rate range of 10.0% to 10.9% as of June 1987.

Table 6.3 Typical Interest Rates (6/87)

Rate Range	Number of Respondents	Percent
Under 10%	0	0
10.0%-10.9%	11	68.8
11.0%-11.9%	3	18.8
Over 12%	2	12.5
Total	16	100

Debt coverage ratios are used by lenders to determine the size of the loan based on the projected cash flow for a club. Survey respondents differed widely on the application of these ratios. A ratio of about 1.15 to 1.20 is considered typical for commercial properties. The median for fitness facilities appears to be at the upper end of this range. Table 6.4 demonstrates the slightly higher risk lenders attach to fitness facilities.

Table 6.4 Typical Debt Coverage Ratios

Debt Coverage Ratios	Number of Respondents	Percent
1.0-1.1	1	6.3
1.11-1.15	1	6.3
1.16-1.20	2	12.5
1.21-1.25	5	31.3
1.26-1.30	5	31.3
1.31+	2	12.5
Total	16	100

Similarly, lenders also recognized higher risk for fitness facilities by offering terms with relatively short call periods. None of the respondents provided call terms greater than 15 years, and over 60% offered terms of 5 years or less. The call term is distinct from the amortization period. Given the relatively short call periods, owners of fitness facilities must obtain refinancing more often than owners of other investment property types. These shorter terms, while providing more protection for lenders, actually contribute to the uncertainty of health club operations and result in higher loan fee costs over the economic life of the facility.

Table 6.5 Typical Call Terms

Loan Term—Years	Number of Respondents	Percent
5 or below	10	62.5
6-9	4	25.0
10-15	2	12.5
16 & over	0	0.0
Total	16	100

Financing costs, otherwise known as fees or points, showed a range between 1% and 3% with a median between 1.6% and 2%. This range may be slightly lower than the average for all commercial properties, which is considered about 2%. These slightly lower fees may reflect the relatively short call terms. The variation of the fees reflects the inexperience of lenders and the inconsistencies of practice in this field.

Table 6.6 Typical Financing Fees/Points

Fees/Points	Number of Respondents	Percent
Under 1.0%	0	0.0
1.0%-1.5%	5	31.3
1.6%-2.0%	7	43.8
2.1%-2.5%	1	6.3
2.6%-3.0%	3	18.8
Over 3.1%	0	0.0
Total	16	100

Trends in mortgage lending reveal a strong emphasis on variable rate loans. About 65% of the lenders used these compared to 35% who used fixed rate mortgages. Lenders noted a significant trend toward variable rate mortgages during the past decade. Others observed the shorter call terms for fitness projects as an increasing trend.

Other comments for lenders further underscore their reluctance to lend for fitness facilities. More institutions are requiring greater owner equity and personal guarantees. One respondent best summarized this conservative lending philosophy toward fitness facilities in a single sentence: "Increasing risk in this market is requiring more equity capital, lower loan-to-value ratios, and quicker loan retirement."

Appraisal Considerations

Survey respondents were asked how they felt appraisals could be improved. The available responses to the categories were as follows:

A. Needs major improvement;

B. Needs moderate improvement; and

C. Most appraisals okay as is.

The following list represents the categories, in order, most often selected with response "A" or "B":

1. Better investigation of depth of market;

2. Include a market analysis;

3. Consideration of future competitive projects;

4. Not accept an assignment unless experienced in the field; and

5. Require an independent feasibility study.

The lenders generally agreed that appraisers should do a more adequate job of deriving capitalization rates, using applicable comparables, and supporting income and expense estimates.

Lenders most strongly endorsed the inclusion of a market analysis and consideration of future competitive projects in an appraisal. Both of these aspects are covered in Chapter 7. These survey results indicate that lenders should be favorably disposed toward the market penetration and feasibility analysis techniques described in the next chapter.

Future Mortgage Practices

The most dramatic finding of our survey was that 92.5% of the respondents stated they did not plan to lend for fitness facilities in the future. More than any other result, this response clearly reveals lenders' rejection of this property type.

The survey attempted to discern the reasons behind lenders' conservatism toward recreational facilities. These results are summarized in Table 6.7. An extraordinary 83.9% stated that these facilities are too special purpose in design to draw loans. The only other category mentioned by more than half of respondents was uncertain long-term appeal. Lenders fear that health clubs are a fad.

Table 6.7   Reasons for Not Making Loans for Fitness Facilities

	Number of Respondents	Percent
Too Special-Purpose Design	52	83.9
Uncertain Long-Term Appeal	32	51.6
Questionable Financial Feasibility	30	48.4
Difficult to Judge Management Expertise	29	46.8
Market Too Difficult to Quantify	27	43.5
Too Many Inexperienced Operators/Developers	24	38.7
Market Is or Will Be Overbuilt	20	32.3
No Applications Submitted	8	12.9
Total Respondents	62	100

Questions regarding financial feasibility are most difficult to judge for proposed projects. Lenders generally are more willing to loan to existing profitable operations because expected debt coverage ratios can be assessed with greater certainty.

Lenders' concern about judging management expertise also ranked high in this survey. In fact, 69% stated that they require borrowers to have a professional management organization for the project. This ratio is considered extremely high compared with other service businesses, and it further illustrates lenders' reluctance to finance fitness facilities.

Obviously, this bleak picture of lending practices for fitness facilities begs the question: How can potential borrowers improve their likelihood of obtaining loans for these types of projects? About 71% of the responding lenders would be more readily convinced if the property was easily converted into alternative uses. Although a storefront fitness studio may be easily reconfigured into retail or office uses, single-purpose structures present difficult reuse problems. Racquetball courts, saunas, and swimming pools represent high functional or external obsolescence if the market for health clubs deteriorates significantly. The design of new clubs should stress conversion potential by including features like nonbearing central walls to permit greater flexibility. Expensive plumbing improvements, however, probably represent little salvage value. Similarly, the liquidation value of exercise equipment will represent a significant loss because of the mechanical wear the machines receive and the constantly changing state of the art.

Another suggestion lenders made to borrowers was to require additional collateral or personal guarantees. This recommendation, by 56% of respondents, argues for lower loan-to-value ratios and loan guarantees based on assets external to the fitness facility. Such terms may prove too onerous for many potential borrowers.

Successful Loan Proposals

The survey of lenders graphically illustrates the negative perceptions of the health and fitness industry held by lending institutions. In addition to the hard facts, many respondents included comments like "too 'faddish' for investors" and health clubs "attract 'fast buck artists' and therefore the risks are too high for us." Given these constraints, the fitness facility owner must prepare carefully when requesting a loan for constructing, expanding, acquiring, or refinancing a facility.

The first step is to identify an appropriate lending institution. The most favorable respondents to fitness facilities in our survey were savings and loans/mutual savings banks. These lenders generally are less constrained by internal loan policies than larger institutions. In addition, they may be more attuned to local market needs. Discussion with officials of local or regional lending institutions is a proper first step toward obtaining a loan. Potential borrowers should inquire about the particular loan package requirements of individual lenders.

The most important step is to assemble a complete loan package, and the cornerstone of this package is an appraisal acceptable to a lender. The selected appraiser should be familiar with the particular type of fitness facility and meet certain qualification requirements, such as the designation MAI (Member of the Appraisal Institute) or SREA (Society of Real Estate Appraisers).

The contents of a complete appraisal are discussed in Chapter 9. Briefly, an appraisal for a loan package should minimally include:

- A description of the property being appraised, including the land, building, improvements, and property rights;
- Architectural drawings, if available;
- Photographs of the facility, both internal and external;
- Maps showing the neighborhood, city, and regional location of the subject;
- A market feasibility analysis of area supply and demand;
- Historical operating data (two or three years if available); and
- Cost, income, and sales comparison approaches to value.

The income approach should include an analysis of projected cash flows. These projections should realistically reflect future market conditions based on existing knowledge of supply and demand, including other proposed projects. Aggressive or unrealistic income and expense projections are not well received by lenders.

To complement the cash flow projections in the appraisal, the borrower should prepare a balance sheet. In addition to profit and loss statements, lenders like to examine the equity position and capital contributions. The borrower should include the resumes of critical staff, a credit history, and a personal guarantee, if available. Other documentation related to the club, for example, a title report, a marketing plan, and so forth, is an appropriate part of a complete loan package.

The borrower should prepare to present orally his or her case to the loan officers. During such a session, the potential borrower must be able to answer all questions. Rehearsals with accountants and architects could improve the presentation. Another positive technique is to invite the loan officer to tour personally the subject fitness facility.

If the health club is a money-maker, financing can probably be arranged. Borrowers should be prepared to shop around for a loan, although beginning with the local banker who knows you is the best place to start.

Market
Feasibility
Analysis

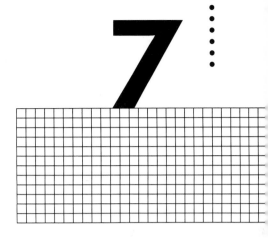

This chapter expands upon the introductory demographic data presented in Chapter 4 and explains the analytical tools necessary to perform a market feasibility analysis. The need for this type of study is evident from the numerous health and fitness projects that have failed in many major metropolitan areas. Although a thorough market analysis may not prevent a club foreclosure, these tools provide the basis for developers, investors, and lenders to evaluate prospective properties and business opportunities.

A market survey provides focused information regarding the competitive environment the subject property faces. Facets of this analysis include identifying market demand and supply characteristics. Market studies are used to determine if sufficient demand is available to support a profitable level of operations for a recreation facility. These conclusions can apply to both the future profitability of existing clubs and the financial feasibility of proposed projects. This framework is a prerequisite for appraising and evaluating all commercial recreation projects in a thorough and complete manner.

A market feasibility study or market analysis is defined as an in-depth examination of an area's supply and demand factors that influence the feasibility of a specific project.

The study should be prepared by an independent, qualified consultant, such as an appraiser/analyst or real estate market research firm. Although a market feasibility study prepared by a developer probably will include relevant data, it generally is unacceptable to a lender because it is viewed as lacking objectivity. Well-documented appraisals should include a detailed market analysis. Independent market research firms and appraisal firms with special expertise are capable of producing good quality market feasibility studies. If separate firms prepare the feasibility and appraisal reports, the monetary and time costs are often high. More efficiency usually is gained by incorporating this effort into a single appraisal assignment.

The benefits of a thorough market feasibility study are numerous; the report can be utilized for several aspects of a project. As part of an appraisal, a market feasibility study helps owners to obtain financing. Lenders are strongly influenced by a well-documented report that will facilitate their decision making. A detailed analysis forces a potential developer or investor to consider the subject property in relation to its competitive environment. Information resulting from the study may aid promotional marketing efforts, help determine appropriate membership rates and fees, and assist with facility planning. The feasibility study also becomes the basis upon which the appraiser projects cash flows and determines value by the income approach.

Project Definition

The first step in a market feasibility study is to identify the specific type of recreation facility to be examined. In most cases, this decision is evident from an inspection of the subject property or a review of architectural drawings. The differentiation between facility types, including design and construction factors, was discussed in Chapter 2. The generic categories include tennis clubs, racquetball clubs, multisport clubs, fitness or aerobics studios, and health spas. These groupings of clubs into recognized categories provide a good basis for analyzing competition according to their sizes, features, and amenities.

The market feasibility analysis envisioned herein is a study that focuses on a specific type of recreational facility. A more open-ended and comprehensive type of feasibility study can be undertaken early in the development process, before a developer has settled on a particular recreational focus or design. This type of study refers to a very comprehensive highest and best use analysis that determines the activities that generate the greatest return or value for a particular parcel of land. Such a preliminary market feasibility study evaluates what type of land use is appropriate and profitable in a given location. After initially determining a commercial recreation use, a detailed study is then needed to evaluate more specifically the chosen alternative.

Target Market Area Identification

As discussed in Chapter 3, the specific location of an existing facility or the selection of a site for a proposed project will determine to a large extent the target market area for the subject. People who join health/fitness clubs value their convenience over most other characteristics of the facility. This conclusion is evident from a large body of survey data on the characteristics of club members. Although the survey did not encompass all types of recreational facilities included in this book, it provides the best basis known to the authors for extrapolating projections of membership data for a specific club.

The referenced survey, commissioned by IRSA and published in 1984, surveyed 22 tennis, racquet, and multisport clubs in the New England, Mideast, Southwest, Southeast, and Great Lakes regions in the United States.[1] Admittedly, this survey did not include any clubs from the Northwest. The total membership of the 22 clubs was 29,363, which provides a substantial basis for reliability. The study examined the demographic characteristics of the members and relevant 1980 U.S. Census data by census tract of the members' residences. Financial operating statistics of the participating clubs also were examined. These figures showed that 20 of the 22 clubs were profitable, and, according to the study's authors, the remaining two clubs had excellent potential for future profitability. Thus, conclusions drawn from this study should be applicable to the successful operations of a given subject club.

The validity of extrapolating the conclusions of this study to other clubs deserves more comment here. In addition to omitting facilities in the Northwest, the study only surveyed clubs that included racquet sport courts either as the primary focus (13 of 22 clubs) or as part of a multisport facility. Thus, the appraiser or analyst should carefully scrutinize the applicability of this analysis to fitness studios, health spas, and special niche fitness facilities. Nonetheless, it would appear that some of the reasoning processes used herein may assist market feasibility analyses of these types of facilities, too. Another consideration is the validity of such extrapolations on a purely mathematical level. Sufficient data are not available to perform confidence interval analyses to insure statistical reliability within a measurable margin of error. Despite these constraints, this guide to a quantifiable market analysis is a powerful tool. It provides the analyst with valuable insights regarding the potential feasibility of a health/fitness club.

The trade area for a club is strongly influenced by members' preference for convenience. As a general rule of thumb, appraisers have considered a 15-minute average driving time as the standard for defining a travel radius. Observations from many markets have not revealed substantial loyalty to any particular club. Yet, if a facility has particularly desirable features, members may travel longer durations to use them. A problem arises as soon as a competing project with comparable amenities is constructed; many existing members can be expected to change to the club in the more convenient location.

Survey data from IRSA on the distance members live from clubs are summarized in Table 3.1. These figures illustrate varying radii that were necessary for clubs to achieve 50%, 60%, 70%, 80%, and 90% membership levels. For racquet, tennis, and multisport clubs at the 50% membership level, the average radius was 5.6 miles and the variation was relatively small, ranging from 5.5 miles to 5.9 miles. This conclusion means that 50% of the members of the surveyed clubs reside within 5.6 miles of the facilities. Table 3.1 shows that very few members live farther than 11.2 miles from the surveyed clubs.

The study also found that racquet sport clubs may have a broader geographic appeal than other health clubs. One explanation may be that members are willing to spend more time traveling to clubs with tennis, squash, and racquetball courts because proportionately fewer clubs with these facilities are available compared with other health clubs.

Defining the target market area has a profound effect on subsequent aspects of the market analysis. These processes include examining demographic variables that influence market demand and determining the locations of competitive facilities. These topics are discussed in the following sections.

Market Demand Analysis

The analysis techniques presented below are designed to quantify market demand for health/fitness/racquet clubs. For this analysis to produce useful results, the appraiser or analyst must have access to high quality demographic data. One of the most comprehensive sources of reliable data is available from the U.S. Census. Because the census is taken only once per decade, the data must be extrapolated to produce more current and applicable bases for analysis. Local governmental agencies and chambers of commerce also are potential sources of demographic data, but nationwide service firms, such as National Planning Data Corporation, National Decision Systems, Public Demographics, Inc. and CACI, offer data in easily used and tailored formats. Many of these services are accessible by a computer with a telephone modem. Demographic data available commercially will require a fee, but these services provide convenient current year estimates and projections.

The most important demographic variables that have been analyzed for fitness club members are population, age, household income, and employment in managerial and professional occupations. The relevance of these variables, based on data from the IRSA survey, is discussed in the following paragraphs.

Population

Table 7.1 shows relevant populations of the areas surrounding the surveyed clubs corresponding to the 50%, 60%, 70%, and 80% membership levels. For the average of all clubs at the 50% membership level, these data reveal that members constitute 0.78% of the general population within a 5.6 mile radius of the subject. This conclusion is based on a large sample that encompassed over 17,600 members and a general population of over 2.2 million people. In addition, the variation of percentages between categories of clubs is relatively small for the population variable.

Table 7.1 Relationship of Club Membership to Market Area Population

	Distance Miles	Members	Population	Mem./ Pop.
NO. CLUBS AT 50%				
6 Racquet Clubs	5.5	5,312	792,602	.67
7 Tennis Clubs	5.9	4,288	475,832	.90
9 Multisport	5.5	8,009	992,890	.81
TOTAL 22 CLUBS	5.6	17,609	2,261,324	.78%
NO. CLUBS AT 60%				
6 Racquet Clubs	7.0	5,910	920,648	.64
7 Tennis Clubs	6.7	4,756	553,578	.85
9 Multisport	6.2	9,858	1,530,224	.64
TOTAL 22 CLUBS	6.6	20,524	3,004,450	.68%
NO. CLUBS AT 70%				
6 Racquet Clubs	7.9	6,563	1,194,384	.55
7 Tennis Clubs	7.6	5,123	820,526	.62
9 Multisport	7.0	10,176	1,718,972	.59
TOTAL 22 CLUBS	7.4	21,862	3,733,882	.59%
NO. CLUBS AT 80%				
6 Racquet Clubs	9.0	7,390	1,838,430	.40
7 Tennis Clubs	8.6	5,497	1,005,639	.55
7 Multisport	8.2	11,063	2,302,779	.48
TOTAL 20 CLUBS	8.6	23,950	5,146,848	.47%

Source: Ron Lawrence, *Club Location—A Site Analysis Study* (Brookline: IRSA, 1984), 21-22.

Age

The correlation between membership and the 25 to 34 age bracket is much stronger than overall population figures. Nationwide surveys reveal that 39% of health club members are between the ages of 24 and 35 compared with 17% of the nationwide population in 1985. Similarly, 31% of members are between the ages of 35 and 44 compared with 18% of the national population.[2] The proportions of members to the population aged 25 to 34 living within the areas of specified percentages of membership are shown in Table 7.2. These data demonstrate that members represent 4.10% of the 25 to 34 population at the 50% membership level. Members of multisport clubs tend to comprise a smaller proportion of the 25 to 34 population (3.16% at the 50% level) than do members of tennis clubs (5.88%). Median age data are included so readers can compare the area data for the surveyed clubs with their own subject markets.

Table 7.2   Club Membership As a Proportion of the Age 25 to 34 Population

	Distance Miles	Members	Pop. 25-34	Mem.%/ Pop. 25-34	Med. Age
NO. CLUBS AT 50%					
6 Racquet Clubs	5.5	5,312	128,701	4.13	36.7
7 Tennis Clubs	5.9	4,288	73,711	5.82	33.9
9 Multisport	5.5	8,009	227,198	3.53	33.9
TOTAL 22 CLUBS	5.6	17,609	429,610	4.10%	34.9
NO. CLUBS AT 60%					
6 Racquet Clubs	7.0	5,910	151,295	3.91	36.1
7 Tennis Clubs	6.7	4,756	87,121	5.45	33.5
9 Multisport	6.2	9,858	347,249	2.84	34.0
TOTAL 22 CLUBS	6.6	20,524	585,665	3.50%	34.6
NO. CLUBS AT 70%					
6 Racquet Clubs	7.9	6,563	199,499	3.29	34.8
7 Tennis Clubs	7.6	5,123	131,030	3.91	33.5
9 Multisport	7.0	10,176	382,402	2.66	35.5
TOTAL 22 CLUBS	7.4	21,862	712,931	3.07%	34.8
NO. CLUBS AT 80%					
6 Racquet Clubs	9.0	7,390	322,032	2.29	33.2
7 Tennis Clubs	8.6	5,497	163,230	3.37	33.3
7 Multisport	8.2	11,063	507,899	2.18	34.9
TOTAL 20 CLUBS	8.6	23,950	993,161	2.41%	34.0

Source: Ron Lawrence, *Club Location—A Site Analysis Study* (Brookline: IRSA, 1984), 21-22.

Household Income

Health club members tend not only to be younger, but also to have greater incomes than the general population. According to the IRSA survey, about 77% of club members' households had incomes greater than $25,000 compared with 61% of households nationwide in 1985. Whereas 32% of all households had incomes over $45,000, 39% of members' households did. Considering that members are relatively younger than the overall population and that they have not yet reached their prime earning years, this finding is even more impressive.[3] At the 50% membership level, the ratio of all club members to households with incomes greater than $25,000 was 4.63%. Higher household incomes, but not per capita incomes, were observed in the market areas for tennis clubs in comparison with market areas for other fitness facilities. These data are summarized in Table 7.3.

Table 7.3 Club Market Area Income Characteristics

	Distance Miles	Members	H.H. W/Inc. >$25K	Mem.% H.H. W/ Inc. W/ 25K	Med. Income	Per Capita Income
NO. CLUBS AT 50%						
6 Racquet Clubs	5.5	5,312	111,708	4.76	23,536	9,857
7 Tennis Clubs	5.9	4,288	65,776	6.52	27,254	9,703
9 Multisport	5.5	8,009	203,221	3.94	22,317	13,331
TOTAL 22 CLUBS	5.6	17,609	380,705	4.63%	$23,600	$11,350
NO. CLUBS AT 60%						
6 Racquet Clubs	7.0	5,910	134,022	4.41	23,746	10,002
7 Tennis Clubs	6.7	4,756	80,895	5.87	28,142	10,249
9 Multisport	6.2	9,858	299,054	3.30	22,070	13,360
TOTAL 22 CLUBS	6.6	20,524	513,971	3.99%	$23,472	$11,750
NO. CLUBS AT 70%						
6 Racquet Clubs	7.9	6,563	168,595	3.89	22,832	9,548
7 Tennis Clubs	7.6	5,123	109,357	4.68	24,538	9,388
9 Multisport	7.0	10,176	327,475	3.11	22,840	13,390
TOTAL 22 CLUBS	7.4	21,862	605,427	3.61%	$23,163	$11,282
NO. CLUBS AT 80%						
6 Racquet Clubs	9.0	7,390	249,350	2.96	22,699	9,417
7 Tennis Clubs	8.6	5,497	132,095	4.16	23,260	9,212
7 Multisport	8.2	11,063	424,346	2.61	22,281	12,814
TOTAL 20 CLUBS	8.6	23,950	805,791	2.97%	$22,589	$10,897

Source: Ron Lawrence, *Club Location—A Site Analysis Study* (Brookline: IRSA, 1984), 21-22.

The IRSA survey relied on 1980 Census data for compiling demographic characteristics of the surveyed clubs' market areas. Although this information is deemed reasonably reliable for most of the other variables, data on household income were based on 1979 tax returns. Median household incomes in the United States have increased dramatically in the 1980s, from $16,461 in 1979 to $23,618 in 1985.[4] Analysts using the IRSA survey data may be advised to increase the basis for the household income variable above $25,000.

Managerial and Professional Employees

Another characteristic of health club members that distinguishes them from the overall population is their type of employment. Similar to the income and age characteristics, a larger proportion of managerial and professional employees are health club members than is true for other employment categories. Table 7.4 illustrates the proportions of members to the number of managerial and professional employees within their respective market areas. At the 50% membership level, the average ratio of members to these employees is 4.03%. Similar to the age and income variables, tennis club members represent a higher proportion of management and professional employees (5.88% at the 50% membership level) than do members of multisport clubs (3.16%).

Table 7.4 Ratio of Club Membership to Managerial and Professional Employees

	Distance Miles	Members	No. Mgr. & Prof.	Mem. % No. Mgr. & Prof. Emply	No. Employed
NO. CLUBS AT 50%					
6 Racquet Clubs	5.5	5,312	110,234	4.82	387,907
7 Tennis Clubs	5.9	4,288	72,961	5.88	221,929
9 Multisport	5.5	8,009	253,611	3.16	560,849
TOTAL 22 CLUBS	5.6	17,609	436,806	4.03%	1,170,685
NO. CLUBS AT 60%					
6 Racquet Clubs	7.0	5,910	135,152	4.37	454,767
7 Tennis Clubs	6.7	4,756	90,074	5.28	257,236
9 Multisport	6.2	9,858	376,103	2.62	850,973
TOTAL 22 CLUBS	6.6	20,524	601,329	3.41%	1,562,976
NO. CLUBS AT 70%					
6 Racquet Clubs	7.9	6,563	164,639	3.99	586,196
7 Tennis Clubs	7.6	5,123	121,612	4.21	371,167
9 Multisport	7.0	10,176	407,386	2.50	942,927
TOTAL 22 CLUBS	7.4	21,862	693,637	3.15%	1,900,290
NO. CLUBS AT 80%					
6 Racquet Clubs	9.0	7,390	249,754	2.96	910,867
7 Tennis Clubs	8.6	5,497	148,836	3.69	454,241
7 Multisport	8.2	11,063	543,452	2.04	1,245,099
TOTAL 20 CLUBS	8.6	23,950	942,042	2.54%	2,610,207

Source: Ron Lawrence, *Club Location—A Site Analysis Study* (Brookline: IRSA, 1984), 21-22.

Market Supply Investigation

The potential profitability of a club is linked to its competitive environment. Loyalty to specific clubs has been weak; should a new club enter a market area, existing clubs can expect to suffer. Thus, the appraiser must identify all existing and proposed competitive facilities to determine the approximate supply/demand balance in a market area. This analysis also may reveal untapped market segments that could be filled through renovation, expansion, or new development.

Identification of Existing and Proposed Competition

The initial segment of the market feasibility analysis, which identified the target market area and the recreational facility type, becomes the framework for researching competitive facilities. In terms of a supply analysis, the target market area within a 6-mile radius of the subject property usually serves as the primary market area. The secondary market area should circumscribe about a 12-mile radius. These figures are approximate and vary depending on the traffic routes and geography of a particular market area. The appraiser or analyst must use judgment to determine what competitive facilities to include in the analysis. For example, a densely populated urban city will require analyzing a smaller area than would be done in a suburban town. If the most similar competitive facility is located 13 miles from the subject, an objective analysis must consider the effect on the market of this competitor.

In any market area, the likelihood of two clubs being identical is remote. Because health and fitness clubs vary in terms of their physical characteristics and amenities, the appraiser or analyst must adopt a somewhat loose definition of "competitive." As an initial step in this process, identify all existing recreational clubs. If the primary focus of the subject is tennis or racquetball, this feature can become the litmus test for identifying potential competitors. For fitness clubs without racquet sports, the inverse of this criteria can be used similarly. In other cases, size of the facility or availability of a pool may prove compelling. The appraiser should recognize that potential members can satisfy their health and fitness needs through a variety of facility types, unless a particular sport is of paramount importance for them.

Existing competitive health clubs provide the best direct market evidence for projecting the feasibility of the subject. Proposed competitive projects, though they will influence the market acceptance of the subject, have yet to be tested in the market themselves. Existing facilities often are identified from the following sources:

- the yellow pages;
- local chambers of commerce;
- local newspapers and magazine advertisements;
- national fitness organizations, including:

    International Racquet Sports Association (IRSA)
    Association of Physical Fitness Centers (APFC)

International Physical Fitness Association (IPFA); and

- other competitive facilities

Once the potential competitive clubs in the market area are identified, the appraiser should visit each facility. A checklist of data to obtain during a tour of recreation facilities is provided in Exhibit 7.5.

Equally important is the identification of proposed competition. New clubs can greatly impact the market penetration and, ultimately, the success or failure of the subject. Obtaining information about potential future competition often is difficult. One of the best sources is local planning or building department officials. Here, the appraiser may be able to review building plans and learn whom to contact regarding a particular development. Other sources may include the client developer, competing developers, or other club owners.

As part of investigating proposed competition, the appraiser should try to determine when the facility will open or if it will be constructed. These considerations are difficult to evaluate because financing or marketing uncertainties can delay or sometimes kill a project. Because objective information is difficult to acquire, a worst-case scenario should be adopted that assumes all or most proposed competition will be built.

Comparison of Subject to Competition

Conducting a market analysis of competitive properties is most productive when the properties are compared directly to the subject. Key comparative data include the size (in square feet) of competitive clubs, annual membership fees or court fees, types of facilities, amenities, year of construction or renovation, and quality. Characteristics of competitive facilities can be arrayed by a range (highest to lowest), average or mean, and most comparable basis to the subject. Individual location and quality characteristics can be rated on a scale (5=excellent, 4=good, 3=average, 2=below average, 1=unacceptable) to arrive at a quantitative evaluation of the competition. Locational characteristics include access and proximity to complementary recreational, retail, and cultural facilities. Aspects related to quality encompass project construction, design, appearance, and amenities.

These comparisons will help place the subject relative to its competitive environment. The goal of comparing the subject to other projects is, first, to identify an overcrowded or unfilled market and,

Exhibit 7.5   Checklist for Inspections of Comparable Clubs

Facility Name _____

Address _____

Manager Name _____

Phone Number _____

Distance from Subject: Miles _____   Minutes _____

Year Built: _____

Year Renovated: _____

Site Description:

Quality of Neighborhood

Proximity to:

   Services   _____

   Retail   _____

   Transit   _____

   Major Employment Centers   _____

   Other Competitors   _____

Comments: _____

_____

_____

Improvement Description:

        Courts: Indoor Tennis   _____

                  Outdoor Tennis   _____

                  Racquetball   _____

                  Squash/Handball   _____

Indoor Size in Square Feet _____

Nautilus or Resistance Machines   _____

Free Weights   _____

Other Athletic Facilities   _____

Dining Facilities   _____

   Seating Capacity   _____

Sauna   _____

Steam   _____

Jaccuzi   _____

Other Amenities   _____

Parking Spaces   _____

Services:

Tennis Lessons   _____

Aerobics Classes   _____

Weight Training   _____

Fitness Testing   _____

Childcare   _____

Other   _____

Market Data:

Hours of Operation   _____

Number of Members   _____

Stated Membership Capacity   _____

Initiation Fees:

     Family   _____

     Single   _____

     Other   _____

Dues or Monthly Fees:

     Family   _____

     Single   _____

     Other   _____

Other Income:

Estimated Total Income:

Estimated Expenses:

Remarks:

second, to estimate an appropriate fee structure or market rent for the subject.

Market Penetration Analysis

Market penetration analysis is a method of estimating the overall market saturation of commercial recreational or health clubs within a market area. It is used to measure the degree to which a market is overbuilt or is fertile for a subject club. This calculation assists the sponsor, lender, appraiser, and consultant in estimating the project's feasibility, its market rent or fee, and its absorption rate and pattern.

Market penetration analysis involves:

- Measuring the theoretical size of the subject's target market;
- Determining the total size of the competitive health club market;
- Calculating the total market penetration ratios for the market area using all proposed and existing comparable facilities (with and without the subject); and
- Evaluating the overall feasibility of the subject given the calculated market penetration rates.

The first step involves summarizing the demographic characteristics discussed under market demand, which provide the basis for estimating the theoretical size of a target market. These variables, which are general population, population aged 25 to 34, households with incomes greater than $25,000, and management and professional employees, have been described in detail. Appropriate sizes of market areas are determined in terms of a radius surrounding the subject in miles, travel time, census tracts, or zip codes. The defined market area should reasonably encompass the relevant competition while utilizing an accessible basis for obtaining demographic data.

Analysts may choose to use different combinations of variables, and even market areas, for calculating penetration rates. All of the variables discussed in this text have validity for measuring demand for health and fitness clubs. Other variables also may be considered, such as the number of occupied households or owner-occupied households, depending on the availability of data. Benchmarks for utilizing other variables, however, are not provided in this book. If adequate local survey data are available, the analyst should not hesitate to devise more specific means for assessing market penetration using these alternate data bases.

The second step is to determine the total size of all existing and proposed competitive clubs. Common methods for measuring competition are number of competitive facilities, total square feet of clubs within the market area, number of courts and total existing membership. The latter factor would be less applicable in market areas where projected facilities or expansions could adversely affect the market. Each of these components—number of courts, square feet, and membership—are compiled both with and without the subject. This step is particularly important if the subject is a proposed club or one that anticipates a physical expansion.

Third, the appraiser or analyst calculates the market penetration rates resulting from all competitive facilities within the subject's market area. This calculation is performed both with and without the subject. The general formula for this calculation is:

$$\text{Market Penetration Rate} = \frac{\text{Total Existing \& Proposed Competition (with and without subject)}}{\text{Market Demand Variable}}$$

Before describing the fourth step, which is analyzing the overall feasibility of the subject, the use and applicability of this formula are explained. This analytical technique allows very liberal applications in terms of the different supply and demand variables it can encompass. Market penetration analysis provides flexibility that should excite appraisers—the analysis becomes the vehicle for systematically organizing and presenting a diverse body of information in a coherent and meaningful manner.

Benchmark Market Penetration Rates

This subsection presents market penetration rates that have been derived from survey data published by IRSA. These rates provide a useful tool for market feasibility analysts to compare market data relevant to their subjects with averages from a nationwide sample of clubs. Appraisers and analysts should exercise caution, however, when using these benchmark ratios. The differences between the physical attributes of the surveyed clubs and the subject may be great, thus reducing the degree of comparability and the confidence of drawing firm conclusions. Useful insight may be evident from a comparison of the average facilities in the surveyed clubs with those of a particular subject. A summary of the physical characteristics and membership of the surveyed clubs is illustrated in Table 7.6.

Table 7.6 Summary of Physical Characteristics and Membership of Surveyed Clubs

Number Surveyed	Type of Club	Average Size/ Sq. Ft.	Average No. of Courts	Average Membership	Average Members Per Court	Average Members/ 1,000 Sq. Ft.
6	Racquet	24,500	12	1,478	123	60
7	Tennis	46,500*	8**	938	117	20
9	Multisport	53,700	14***	1,547	111	29
22	All Clubs	43,900	11	1,335	121	30

* Indoor square footage.

** Includes an average of 6 indoor and 2 outdoor courts.

*** Includes an average of 9 tennis and 5 racquet courts.

Source: Ron Lawrence, "Club Location—Setting Your Sights on the Right Site," *Club Business* (Brookline: IRSA, April 1984), p. 24.

Table 7.6 shows the average sizes of the surveyed clubs in terms of their square footage, number of courts, and membership. Comparison ratios are also illustrated for average members per court and average members per 1,000 square feet of indoor club area. The average number of members per court for the various types of clubs shows remarkably little variation, from 111 to 123, a difference of about 11%. The average membership per 1,000 square feet of club area demonstrates very wide variation, from 20 to 60, a difference of 300%! Purely racquetball clubs are typically the smallest facilities in terms of area, but they have a greater number of members per court than other clubs with courts. Tennis clubs generally require the fewest members per court for profitable operation.

The ratios describing the characteristics of the surveyed clubs, combined with data about competitive clubs in the market areas of these clubs, provide the basis for developing benchmark market penetration rates. Shown in Table 7.7 are market penetration rates based on the number of competitive clubs. This table considers the total number of clubs, that is, the IRSA member clubs that participated in the survey plus competitive clubs, located within the specified market areas. The numbers of clubs were divided into the total demand variables (general population, population aged 25 to 34, households with incomes greater than $25,000, and managerial and professional employees) within the corresponding market areas to derive the market penetration rates. These penetration ratios are considered benchmarks for comparison with rates derived for particular subject clubs. A hypothetical example at the end of this section illustrates a potential application of this analytical tool.

The next set of benchmark penetration rates is presented in Table 7.8. This table was developed in much the same way as Table 7.7, except that the per-competitive-club data were adjusted for the average sizes of the surveyed facilities. The IRSA survey only included size data for the 22 member clubs and not the competing clubs in the market area. In order to develop penetration rates on a more sophisticated level than a per club basis, the authors have made the assumption that the average competitive club in the IRSA survey resembled the characteristics of the surveyed clubs. On the basis of averages for all fitness facilities, common sense indicates that clubs with larger facilities have more courts, members, and gross revenues than those with smaller facilities. Although many exceptions are evident in the market, average industry-wide data provide reasonable support for this assumption.

Market penetration rates based on the total size of competitive facilities in the market area provide a superior analytical tool to rates based on the gross number of competitors. For example, a market area with a small number of large clubs or a large number of small clubs may result in skewed penetration rates derived on a per club basis. Adjusting these same rates for a particular market area based on the total floor area of the competitive clubs probably would yield more meaningful results. This point is illustrated in the following hypothetical example.

Market Penetration Rates in Practice

The theoretical discussion above is easier to comprehend when placed in the context of a concrete example. This hypothetical case study is an abbreviated description of a more detailed investigation and analysis that would be necessary in a complete market penetration study. The purpose is to illustrate the basic principles of using the market penetration ratios provided above.

Table 7.7 Benchmark Market Penetration Rates—Per Competitive Club

Ratios	Distance In Miles	Pop % Competitors	Pop 25%-34% Competitors	No. of Households Income >25K% Competitors	No. Mgr. & Prof. Employees % Competitors
AT 50%					
6 Racquet Clubs	5.5	44,033	7,150	6,206	6,124
7 Tennis Clubs	5.9	31,722	4,914	4,385	4,864
9 Multisport Clubs	5.5	33,096	7,573	6,774	8,454
TOTAL 22 CLUBS	5.6	35,894	6,819	6,043	6,933
AT 60%					
6 Racquet Clubs	7.0	46,036	7,565	6,701	6,758
7 Tennis Clubs	6.7	30,754	4,840	4,494	5,004
9 Multisport Clubs	6.2	49,362	11,201	9,647	12,132
TOTAL 22 CLUBS	6.6	43,543	8,488	7,449	8,715
AT 70%					
6 Racquet Clubs	7.9	54,290	9,068	7,663	7,484
7 Tennis Clubs	7.6	45,585	7,279	6,075	6,756
9 Multisport Clubs	7.0	46,458	10,335	8,851	11,010
TOTAL 22 CLUBS	7.4	48,492	9,259	7,863	9,008
AT 80%					
6 Racquet Clubs	9.0	76,601	13,418	10,390	10,406
7 Tennis Clubs	8.6	52,928	8,591	6,952	7,833
7 Multisport Clubs	8.2	52,336	11,543	9,644	12,351
TOTAL 20 CLUBS	8.6	59,159	11,416	9,262	10,828

Source: Ron Lawrence, Club Location—Setting Your Sites on the Right Site," *Club Business* (Brookline: IRSA, April 1984), p. 25.

Table 7.8 Benchmark Market Penetration Rates—Per 1,000 Square Feet of Club Area

Ratios	Distance in Miles	Pop % Competitors	Pop 25%-34% Competitors	No. of Households With Incomes Over $25,000 % Competitors	Number of Mgr. & Prof. Employees % Competitors
AT 50%					
6 Racquet Clubs	5.5	1,797	670	253	250
7 Tennis Clubs	5.9	682	106	94	105
9 Multisport Clubs	5.5	616	141	126	157
TOTAL 22 CLUBS	5.6	818	155	138	158
AT 60%					
6 Racquet Clubs	7.0	1,879	309	274	276
7 Tennis Clubs	6.7	661	104	97	108
9 Multisport Clubs	6.2	919	209	180	226
TOTAL 22 CLUBS	6.6	992	193	170	199
AT 70%					
6 Racquet Clubs	7.9	2,216	370	313	305
7 Tennis Clubs	7.6	980	157	131	145
9 Multisport Clubs	7.0	865	192	165	205
TOTAL 22 CLUBS	7.4	1,105	211	179	205
AT 80%					
6 Racquet Clubs	9.0	3,127	548	424	425
7 Tennis Clubs	8.6	1,138	185	150	168
7 Multisport Clubs	8.2	975	215	180	230
TOTAL 20 CLUBS	8.6	1,348	260	211	247

These penetration ratios assume that average club size (24,500 square feet for racquetball clubs, 46,500 square feet for tennis clubs, 53,700 square feet for multisport clubs, and 43,900 square feet for all clubs) determined for the 22 surveyed IRSA clubs are applicable to the average sizes for the 77 competitive clubs (99 clubs including the IRSA clubs) in the same market areas.

Source: Derived from data published by IRSA, 1984.

This hypothetical example attempts to determine whether a new health club containing 50,000 square feet should be built. A 6.6 mile radius of analysis has been selected, which corresponds with the 60% membership level in Table 3.1. Within this area, the analyst has discovered four comparable competitive clubs containing a total of 205,000 square feet. The demographic characteristics of this market area are summarized as follows:

Population	200,000
Age 25 to 34 population	38,000
Households with income greater than $25,000	35,000
Managerial and professional employees	41,000

The market penetration analysis on a per competitive club basis is illustrated in Table 7.9. The benchmark ratios are from Table 7.7 and correspond with the 60% membership level for the average of all clubs. The ratios for the existing and proposed markets were calculated by dividing 4 and 5, respectively, into the demographic characteristic variables of this market area. The percentage difference columns range from about +12% to +18% for the existing market and −6% to −10% for the proposed market. In general, positive percentage differences, that is, calculated market penetration ratios greater than the benchmark figures, indicate the potential for supply expansion in the market. Conversely, negative percentage differences, or calculated penetration ratios lower than the benchmark figures, indicate that a market may be overbuilt.

The general conclusion, that is, not to add a new club in the hypothetical market based on the per club penetration ratios, is more clearly illustrated through an examination of club sizes. This analysis is summarized in Table 7.10. These ratios were calculated in the same manner as those in Table 7.9, except the denominators were based on the total building areas of the clubs in the market area—205,000 square feet for the existing market and 255,000 square feet for the proposed market. The resulting percentage differences for the existing market range from about −4% to +1%. These percentages are very close to zero and indicate that the market is in approximate equilibrium based on the sizes of the competitive clubs. This finding is demonstrated more dramatically when the proposed 50,000 square foot facility is added. The resulting penetration ratios are substantially below the benchmark ratios, as evidenced by the substantial negative percentage differences ranging from about −19% to −23%.

Table 7.9 Hypothetical Penetration Analysis Based on Numbers of Competitive Properties

Demographic Variables	Benchmark Penetration @ 60% Membership (Per Club Basis)	Existing Market (4 Clubs)	Percentage Difference W/Benchmark	Proposed Market (5 Clubs)	Percentage Difference W/Benchmark
Population Age 25-34	43,543	50,000	+14.8%	40,000	− 8.1%
Population Household Income over $25K	8,488	9,500	+11.9%	7,600	−10.5%
Managerial & Professional	7,449	8,750	+17.5%	7,000	− 6.0%
Employees	8,715	10,250	+17.6%	8,200	− 5.9%

A byproduct of the hypothetical example is that the clubs in this market are larger than the average size of those in the IRSA survey. Furthermore, this analysis assumes that the relative operating success of all competitive clubs is approximately equal.

Analysts using the percentage differences technique illustrated above must exercise caution and judgment before drawing firm conclusions. The author of the IRSA survey, Ron Lawrence of Market Resources, Inc., has written that a well-located club may be able to compete successfully in a market that appears overbuilt.[5] Existing competitive clubs may be clustered in a small geographic segment of the market area while another location may be more convenient for a large body of potential members. A scenario is possible where the new club, located in the underserved submarket, will succeed while one or two marginal existing clubs may close their doors.

Determining Overall Feasibility

The fourth step in the market penetration analysis is to evaluate the market penetration ratios and analyze a club's overall feasibility. In the simplified hypothetical example above, the indication of whether the market would support an additional club seemed clear. Because the market penetration ratios were below the benchmark figures, sufficient justification for a new club was not available. If the proposed club, however, had a clearly superior location in relation to its competitors, then it could possibly succeed. If the percentage differences between the benchmark rates and the calculated rates were only slightly negative and the relevant demographic variables in the market area were projected to grow significantly, the analyst also might have concluded that the new club was justified.

These examples of qualifying considerations, in the light of negative conclusions from the market penetration ratios analysis, illustrate the complexity of a feasibility study. Not only must the analyst examine quantifiable factors, but also subjective considerations. For example, will the addition of a pool improve membership? Will it enable the imposition of a higher fee structure?

A market penetration analysis cannot specifically consider particular advantages or deficiencies that a project may offer. A positive or negative market penetration rate will not guarantee the success or failure of a club. The financial operations of a club are greatly influenced by its quality, location, marketing efforts, and management. In addition, market

Table 7.10 Hypothetical Penetration Analysis Based on Sizes of Competitive Clubs

Demographic Variables	Benchmark Penetration @ 60% Membership (Per 1,000 Sq. Ft. Basis)	Existing Market (205,000 Sq. Ft.)	Percentage Difference W/Benchmark	Proposed Market (255,000 Sq. Ft.)	Percentage Difference W/Benchmark
Population Age 25-34	992	976	−1.6%	784	−21.0%
Population Household Income over $25K	193	185	−4.1%	149	−22.8%
Managerial & Professional Employees	170	171	+0.6%	137	−19.4%
	199	200	+0.5%	161	−19.1%

penetration ratios can become meaningless if an appraiser improperly establishes basic information on the market area, demographic characteristics, or competition.

Primary Market Research

Another method for determining market feasibility is to conduct a market survey for a particular market area. The penetration ratio analysis described above relied on readily available secondary data, either from the U.S. Census or other sources. Primary market research incorporates either surveys of randomly selected individuals from the market area, interviews of members of competitive clubs, or focus study groups. These studies can generate specific demand information for the subject's market area that is more reliable than the results of a market penetration analysis based on a nationwide survey of clubs. The drawbacks of primary market research are the monetary and time costs. For these reasons, it is advisable only for very large and high-end recreational clubs.

Survey research involves sampling a target population through mailed questionnaires, telephone interviews, or one-on-one interviews. Of these, questionnaires often produce the highest response rate because of their anonymity. This type of survey also tends to be less expensive to conduct and tabulate. The main objectives of survey research are to estimate market demand, assist with physical structural design, and guide marketing strategies. Surveys typically request the following:

- Where the respondent lives and works;
- If he/she is a member of a club and if so, which one;
- What aspects of the existing club are liked/disliked;
- What facilities are desirable in a club;
- Whether the respondent is considering joining a club; and
- How much the respondent is willing to pay.

Focus study research involves comprehensive questioning of a small group of potential club members or members of competing clubs. The purpose of the focus study is to test the acceptance of the subject's design, amenities, and fees. Another topic may include the respondent's awareness of competitive clubs. The process also could generate word-of-mouth advertising for the subject. These sessions, however, should be open-ended and nonjudgmental. Their focus is information gathering, not high pressure selling.

Financial Feasibility Analysis

Research and analysis performed in a financial feasibility study become the basis for forecasting cash flows from a recreational club. In turn, the appraiser uses these data in the income approach to determine a value for the subject facility. The projections also are useful in determining overall returns on investment, preparing after-debt-service cash flows, and evaluating the riskiness of the investment. These criteria are very important to developers, lenders, and potential buyers.

The financial feasibility study is comprised of income and expense projections. The foundation for these projections is contained in the market feasibility analysis. Although financial forecasting is an imprecise science, the more reliable forecasts are based on direct market evidence. Potential sources of operating data, in their relative order of importance, are:

1. Historical operating statements from the subject club;
2. Surveys of competitors in the subject's market area;
3. Surveys of similar facilities in nearby market areas; and
4. Published industry-wide averages or standards.

These sources generally apply to obtaining both income and expense data. The process of a financial feasibility study, as described in this section, should follow these steps:

determining market fees or rents;
projecting gross revenues;
estimating annual operating expenses;
and forecasting annual cash flows.

Determining Market Fees or Rents

Most clubs base their charge to members on a monthly or annual fee. Periodic dues are the amount a person(s) must pay to a facility for the right to basic membership privileges as defined in the membership contract or application. The structures of these charges vary considerably from club to club and between different market areas. Some of the forms of membership fees and dues are summarized below:

- Duration: annual, monthly, winter, summer;
- Time of day: prime time, nonprime time;
- Class: single, family, couple, student;

- Facility usage: general, tennis, pool, fitness, and so forth; and
- Composition: ranging from heavy emphasis on dues with small or no initiation fees to minimal emphasis on recurring charges and greater up-front costs.

For racquet sports clubs, membership often is segregated between individuals, couples, and families. Thus, one of the goals of market research for appraising these types of clubs is to determine the proportions of types of membership in competitive clubs. A few clubs also differentiate membership fees based on what facilities in the club the member is permitted to use. For example, a club in Minnesota charges monthly unlimited-usage fees of $8 for weight equipment only, $15 for weights and aerobics, and $30 for racquetball.

In addition to monthly dues, many clubs charge substantial initiation fees. These types of fee structures are found in various types of clubs, ranging from deluxe facilities, such as country clubs, to storefront weights and aerobics studios. In the former types of clubs, membership often is limited by the number of available courts, and some successful operations have waiting lists for new members. Storefront operations rely upon the turnover of membership because a high percentage of members discontinue intensive usage within a few months of joining. Thus, annual projections of initiation fees must consider an attrition factor for the subject club.

The primary emphasis in determining market fees is usually placed on the operating history of the subject club. This data source is verified and supplemented through an investigation of fees for comparable facilities located in the subject's market area. Only if these data sources are unavailable or inapplicable should the appraiser rely on comparables outside the immediate market area or on industry-wide averages. Comparisons between the subject and comparables, based on the previously discussed measures of quality, location, physical facilities, and amenities, should guide the appraiser in determining the appropriate market fee structure for the subject.

For leased facilities, a determination of market rent is necessary. In the case of storefront operations and some other clubs, rents usually are stated in terms of dollars and cents per square foot, either per month or per year. A few lease agreements also include a percentage rent clause based on gross or, infrequently, net annual sales. Valuations of these types of properties generally follow the procedures for appraising retail stores. If a business valuation is desired, the procedures outlined herein for estimating revenues and expenses would be applicable.

Projecting Gross Revenues

Revenues attributed to club operations depend to a large extent on the types of facilities a club provides. An obvious example is food and beverage sales. Other examples include tennis lessons, pro shop sales, equipment rental, vending machine sales, swimming fees, locker rental charges, and other usage charges. The charging of separate fees for using particular equipment or facilities, however, does not usually constitute a large portion of revenues. Clubs usually have a membership fee which entitles members to use all facilities.

Departmental revenues are projected using a variety of means. These revenue sources generally are a function of physical features and membership usage. Departmental revenues generally are expressed as an annual dollar amount per member per square foot or per court, or as a percentage of annual membership fees. As a general rule of thumb for multisport clubs, membership dues account for about 70% of total revenues and other sources comprise about 30% of gross income. Clubs without substantive departments generate a higher proportion of revenues from membership dues.

Similar to the policy in determining membership fees, appraisers should rely upon the experience of the subject club and competitive facilities to determine appropriate projections of other income. In practice, obtaining operating income and, as discussed subsequently, expense data from competitive clubs may prove difficult. When good information about other operating income categories is not available from the market, the appraiser may have to rely upon industry averages.

Estimating Annual Operating Expenses

Total operating expenses usually are quoted as a percentage of gross income, as illustrated in Tables 7.11 and 7.12, which show industry averages. For most clubs total operating expenses as a percentage of gross income range from less than 50% to 82%. The former figure is from the "top five clubs" in the IRSA survey and the latter figure is from Robert Morris Associates' figures for health and fitness clubs with assets in excess of $1,000,000 (Standard Industrial Classification Code Number 7299). These ratios are influenced by a variety of factors, including

Table 7.11 Industry Operating Data Published by IRSA for 1986

Multirecreation Clubs with Indoor Pools

	Average Club		Top Five	
	Average Dollars	Ratio to Total Revenues	Average Dollars	Ratio to Total Revenues
Revenues				
Membership Dues and Fees	$1,211,798	70.6%	$1,201,340	73.8%
Racquet Sports	130,380	7.6	164,060	10.1
Pro Shop	48,444	2.8	45,600	2.8
Fitness Center	8,398	.5	9,200	.6
Dance and Exercise	4,250	.2	2,400	.1
Food & Beverage	177,584	10.3	103,800	6.4
Swimming/Whirlpools	4,682	.3	—	—
Rentals	37,869	2.2	67,200	4.1
Other Income	93,107	5.5	34,280	2.1
Total Revenues	1,716,512	100.0	1,627,880	100.0
Direct Operating Costs and Expenses				
Racquet Sports	57,734	3.4	25,380	1.6
Pro Shop	41,312	2.4	34,885	2.1
Fitness Center	48,103	2.8	31,820	2.0
Dance & Exercise	28,842	1.7	22,040	1.4
Food & Beverage	164,767	9.6	76,540	4.7
All Other	16,078	.9	6,020	.3
Total Direct Operating Costs and Expenses	356,836	20.8	196,685	12.1
Income before Indirect Operating Expenses and Fixed Charges	1,359,676	79.2	1,431,195	87.9
Indirect Expenses				
General Repairs and Maintenance	140,847	8.2	105,100	6.5
Energy and Utilities	111,176	6.5	85,040	5.2
Marketing & Sales	89,837	5.2	51,560	3.2
General and Administrative				
Other Payroll, Payroll Taxes, and Employee Benefits Not Deducted Elsewhere	223,062	13.0	97,142	5.9
Other	193,436	11.3	239,615	14.7
Total General and Administrative	416,498	24.3	336,757	20.6
Total Indirect Expenses	758,358	44.2	578,457	35.5
Income before Fixed Charges	601,318	35.0	852,738	52.4
Fixed Charges				
Real Estate and Personal Property Taxes	42,458	2.5	18,280	1.1
Property and Business Interruption Insurance	28,824	1.6	34,099	2.1
Total Fixed Charges	71,282	4.1	52,379	3.2
Income before Rent, Interest, Depreciation, Amortization and Taxes on Income	$ 530,036	30.9%	$ 800,359	49.2%

Source: IRSA, "Profiles of Success—1987 State of the Industry Report," 1987, p. 20.

Table 7.12　Industry Operating Data Published by PKF for 1986

	All City Clubs	Geographic Divisions				Size Classifications (Membership)			
		East	South	Mid-west	Far West	Under 750	750 to 1,500	1,501 to 2,500	Over 2,500
Ratios to Total Income									
Sales and Income—									
Except Dues:									
Food	54.7%	54.0%	69.3%	51.7%	57.9%	59.0%	65.4%	56.2%	46.6%
Beverages	16.2	16.1	15.2	16.7	18.0	17.5	18.0	15.8	15.2
Rooms	12.0	16.2	—	15.2	7.3	11.5	6.1	7.0	19.3
Minor-Operated Depts.	6.9	5.2	10.5	6.5	8.1	2.0	3.0	8.6	9.0
Sports Activities	4.0	3.3	2.5	6.6	3.3	2.8	1.4	3.2	6.3
Other Income	6.2	5.2	2.5	3.3	5.4	7.2	6.1	9.2	3.6
Total Sales and Income	100.0%	100.0%	100.0%	100.0%	100.0%	100.0%	100.0%	100.0%	100.0%
Departmental Expenses:									
Food and Beverages	70.1%	70.7%	65.2%	63.8%	76.7%	74.1%	82.7%	69.5%	62.9%
Rooms	4.9	5.7	—	5.9	4.9	6.6	3.4	2.9	6.8
Minor-Operated Depts.	6.9	5.6	7.4	7.4	8.5	2.6	3.3	8.0	9.1
Sports Activities	4.3	4.7	2.6	6.1	3.6	4.5	1.3	3.3	6.8
Total Departmental Expenses	86.2%	86.7%	75.2%	83.2%	93.7%	87.8%	90.7%	83.7%	85.6%
Net Departmental Income	13.8%	13.3%	24.8%	16.8%	6.3%	12.2%	9.3%	16.3%	14.4%
Less Unapportioned									
Expenses:									
Clubrooms	10.1%	12.1%	12.2%	10.3%	9.3%	7.8%	10.0%	10.2%	10.7%
Entertainment—Net	1.0	.8	.5	1.4	1.5	2.1	1.1	.4	1.2
Administrative and General	21.8	19.2	25.4	19.8	22.0	28.3	25.1	22.0	18.0
Heat, Light, and Power	8.2	9.3	3.5	11.0	6.3	7.2	6.4	6.4	10.9
Repairs and Maintenance	7.8	6.4	4.6	12.7	8.4	7.3	7.4	5.4	10.3
Total Unapportioned Expenses	48.9%	47.8%	46.2%	55.2%	47.5%	52.7%	50.0%	44.4%	51.1%
Net Cost of Operations	35.1%	34.5%	21.4%	38.4%	41.2%	40.5%	40.7%	28.1%	36.7%
Membership Dues	53.3	50.5	41.0	55.4	63.7	56.5	57.7	44.8	57.5
Dues Available for Fixed Charges	18.2%	16.0%	19.6%	17.0%	22.5%	16.0%	17.0%	16.7%	20.8%
Rent, Taxes, and Insurance	10.5	9.7	18.6	9.5	8.5	11.1	12.1	13.1	7.4
Balance of Dues Available for Debt Service, Capital									
Improvements, etc.	7.7%	6.3%	1.0%	7.5%	14.0%	4.9%	4.9%	3.6%	13.4%

Note: Payroll Taxes and Employee Benefits distributed to each department.

Source: Pannell Kerr Forster, "Clubs in Town and Country—1986," p. 17.

location, managerial competence, extent of service provision, project size, and facility types. The categories of operating departments that are included in a facility can significantly affect expense ratios. For example, food and beverage operations in health clubs tend to experience relatively high expense-to-revenue ratios, which usually result in higher overall expense ratios. If beverage departments include a liquor license, however, the expense ratio usually is lower. Appraisers should use caution when applying industry averages for determining operating expense ratios. General rules of thumb should not replace specific line item analysis of operating expenses.

One way to assess operating expenses more rigorously is to disaggregate operating expenses into separately analyzed categories. A basic technique is to divide expenses into fixed and variable categories. Typically, fixed operating expenses include real estate, personal and other property taxes, and property and business insurance. Variable expenses often are divided into direct and indirect categories. Direct variable costs resemble departmental expenses in a hotel or motel. For example, separate accounting categories usually are used for food and beverage and pro shop expenses, if a club has these facilities. Other clubs disaggregate operating expenses attributable to specific operations, such as racquet sports or aerobics. The remaining operating expense categories can be as detailed as data availability permits. Typical indirect operating expense categories include energy, utilities, repairs and maintenance, and administrative and general.

In addition to a percentage analysis of operating expenses, projections often require analyses of specific expenses. Estimates of fixed expenses for property taxes and insurance may be obtainable from appropriate local experts, such as an assessor and an insurance broker. Variable expenses are dependent to a large extent on membership levels. Contacts with local health club operators may reveal the best data. To evaluate operating statistics from comparables, the appraiser must adjust the data to common unit measures. Typical bases include per square foot, per member, and per court.

One of the most critical factors the appraiser must consider in this analysis is adjusting the comparables to the subject based on the similarity or differences in facilities. Some subjective adjustments usually are necessary because the likelihood of obtaining operating data from an identical facility in the same market area is remote. Nonetheless, the adjusted data will form a better basis of comparison with the subject and enable the appraiser to derive a reasonable estimate of operating expenses.

Forecasting Annual Cash Flows

After assembling all the appropriate data for the income and expense categories, the appraiser can calculate net operating income (NOI). NOI is equal to total operating revenues minus all the expense categories: direct operating costs, indirect expenses, and fixed charges plus reserves. This figure, before allowances for interest expense, depreciation, and income taxes, is the basis for determining an estimate of value by income capitalization. This analytical procedure is part of the appraisal process, which is described in the following chapter.

Projections of income and expenses, due to the variable nature of all income and most expenses, depend on membership levels. In the case of an existing facility at a stabilized level of operation, developing projections is relatively easy. Through the market feasibility analysis, knowledge of demographic trends and proposed competition may influence projecting course of future revenues and expenses differently than the existing case normally would indicate.

For proposed facilities, the appraiser must forecast an absorption period for membership sales. Review of numerous appraisals from throughout the country has revealed a variety of techniques for such an analysis. One of the most common is to base membership absorption for subject clubs on the experience of recently opened competitive clubs. Although this method may prove valid in some cases, it has obvious pitfalls. If a market became saturated with the addition of the previous facility, a new facility would not experience the same absorption levels.

The absorption experience of other clubs should be balanced with the market penetration ratios analysis. These figures are good indicators of supply/demand balance in the market. Ratios significantly above the industry averages should indicate a more rapid absorption than ratios moderately or slightly above average.

Membership capacities are estimated using a variety of sources, including industry averages from Table 7.6, experiences of competitive clubs in the market area, and the opinions of the project developer if he/she is experienced in this field. Absorption periods vary greatly, depending on the market, but typically range from 6 to 24 months. Longer absorption periods of up to 48 months are possible in overbuilt markets.

Absorption rates usually are stated in terms of the numbers of members per month or as a percentage of total membership capacity. For example, a multisport club is projected to have a capacity of 1,600 members. A 20-month absorption period would equate to 80 members, or 5%, per month. A proposed facility also is likely to sell some memberships before the facility opens, which could influence the absorption projection. Generally, lenders favor conservative estimates of absorption and pre-opening sales.

Project Feasibility

Determinations of the annual internal rates of return on proposed or existing developments usually are beyond the scope of appraisal assignments. Developers, potential investors, and lenders, however, are concerned about the ability of a business or a real estate project to service its debt service requirements and generate a profit. Ratio analysis incorporates debt service cash flows into the analysis of net operating cash flows to arrive at the information needed for calculating the overall yield rates of a development. The most common ratio to measure overall profitability is the return on investment ratio, which is calculated as follows:

Net cash flow/total equity

where net cash flow is defined as annual cash flow from operations (less annual debt service).

This ratio (also known as "cash on cash" return) can be calculated annually, on a net present value basis, or averaged over the projection period. The calculated return can then be evaluated by the developer according to his or her own risk/return criteria and comparisons to competing investments. Other common project yield ratios include:

- annual net income/total development cost;
- profit (appraisal value less total development cost)/total development cost;
- annual after-tax cash flow/total development cost;
- profit/equity; and
- annual after-tax cash flow/equity.

To evaluate profitability, the developer or sponsor can employ other commonly used financial evaluation techniques, such as net present value analysis (discounted cash flows less total development cost), payback period analysis, and utility/probability analysis. Finally, each of the above techniques for quantifying a project's profitability can incorporate the tax effect of cash flows to each equity participant, or joint venture/syndication equity distributions, as appropriate.

The Appraisal Process

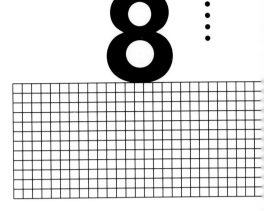

The appraisal of health and fitness clubs can be accomplished through the use of conventionally accepted appraisal principles, methods, and techniques. However, these facilities have special design features and usually include an element of business as well as real estate value. Thus, appraisers must consider these unique factors when valuing both existing or proposed recreational projects.

The types of facilities included in this text may be appraised by the three traditional approaches to value: the cost approach, the sales comparison approach, and the income approach. The basic reference text for application of these approaches is *The Appraisal of Real Estate* (9th edition), published by the American Institute of Real Estate Appraisers. In most cases, the purpose of the appraisal is to estimate market value derived from a reconciliation of the three approaches. As with many sophisticated properties whose revenues are nonrental in nature, appraisals of recreational clubs virtually always include a consideration of the value of the going concern or business. Consequently, a club's worth may be more than just the value of the real estate assets; it includes furniture and equipment, licenses, and the reputation or goodwill established by its operations in the community. Therefore, in a reconciliation of the three approaches, the income approach, which reflects business value, is usually given greatest weight.

This chapter describes the components of an appraisal report. A thorough narrative appraisal will include all of these elements. For some purposes, such as asset management, certain components may be omitted. For lending purposes, however, a complete appraisal almost always is required.

Influences on Value

Regional/City Analysis

The regional description section of the appraisal contains a discussion of geography, political boundaries, population, demographics, housing, employment, economic development, transportation, and cultural data. This information is important in assessing the overall development climate, measuring economic trends, projecting potential demand, and defining the market area for a specific recreational project. Special consideration should be given to current and projected demographic data for the specific variables discussed in Chapter 7: general population, population aged 25 to 34, households with incomes greater than $25,000, and managerial and professional employees. Other factors worthy of consideration include geographic concentrations of population, the extent of existing and proposed competitive recreational facilities, and direction of growth.

To obtain this information, an appraiser should contact local chambers of commerce or economic development departments. Many cities have prepared, either by themselves or with the help of outside consultants, studies of economic and demographic trends to assist with a variety of planning efforts. In other localities, associations of local governments or regional planning agencies may have prepared relevant analyses or projections. Demographic service companies also can provide specific age, population, and income statistics for any defined area.

Neighborhood Analysis

This section of an appraisal reviews existing and proposed development within the immediate area of the subject site. An appraiser can garner information on development trends in a neighborhood through personal inspection and by talking with city officials, developers, and brokers familiar with an area. In analyzing a neighborhood, the appraiser should specifically address the following:

- proximity to major employment centers, concentrations of population, downtown retail and shopping centers, and recreational facilities;
- availability of public transportation;
- access from major thoroughfares and highways; and
- overall neighborhood quality (nature and condition of surrounding structures and public improvements, affluence, rent levels, security, and reputation).

After assessing the strengths and weaknesses of a specific site, the appraiser should draw a conclusion about the desirability of the location for a commercial recreational facility, including a discussion of potential external obsolescence.

Site Description

The site description section in an appraisal contains facts about the site's physical characteristics, existing improvements, access and exposure, assessments and taxes, easements and encumbrances, excess land, and zoning. Appraisers obtain site information through personal inspections; reviews of the subject's public file at city hall or county administrative center; discussions with governmental officials, including assessors; and documents such as the subject's title report.

Description of Improvements

In the improvement description section, the appraiser includes all buildings and improvements relevant to the subject. Appropriate topics include a detailed discussion of facility type, size, construction, and design. A description of facility type should specifically comment on amenities, such as numbers and types of courts, locker and shower facilities, whirlpool, sauna, steam rooms, swimming pools, food and beverage capabilities, landscaping, and parking. Special construction details of health clubs are numerous. Some examples include hardwood floors for racquetball courts and gymnasiums, mirrored wall coverings, and specially cushioned floors for aerobics and dance exercises.

Improvement description detail usually is obtained from a thorough inspection of the subject property. For proposed clubs, appraisers must utilize architectural plans or drawings, discussions with the developer and project architect, and a review of the project's public file.

Finally, the appraiser should discuss whether the construction quality, design, amenities, and landscaping are appropriate for the recreational club. This analysis should identify any physical inadequacies and potential functional depreciation by assessing the strengths and weaknesses of the subject's physical design relative to competitive facilities.

Market Analysis

The market analysis section of the appraisal analyzes the project's market feasibility. The relevant information for this section was described in detail in the previous chapter. Usually, appraisal reports are organized so that pure market data are presented in a separate section while financial operating data are compiled in the income approach. The market feasibility analysis not only provides data for estimating market rents and absorption, but is also instrumental in determining the highest and best use of the site.

The market feasibility study sometimes is prepared before the appraiser is retained and is, therefore, available for the appraiser's use. Although a well-prepared market study can save an appraiser research time, it is still the appraiser's responsibility to assess independently any conclusions or opinions set forth in the study. This assessment includes an analysis of the consultant's research methods and a verification of comparable facility data.

The key step in a market feasibility analysis is investigating the subject's proposed and existing competition. The appraiser should personally inspect and photograph important comparable facilities. Comparable facilities should be discussed briefly and arrayed on a summary grid, as illustrated in Table 8.1.

Highest and Best Use

Highest and best use is defined as that use, from among reasonably probable and legal alternative uses, found to be physically possible and financially feasible that results in maximized land value. This concept also must recognize community environmental and developmental goals in addition to wealth maximization of individual property owners. The highest and best use of a vacant site may be different from the highest and best use of an existing improved property. This scenario is possible when the

Table 8.1 Example of a Survey of Multisport Club Comparables

	Subject	1	2	3	4
Miles from Club	N.A.	6	5	2	30
Initiation Fees	-0-	$350	$350	-0-	$250
Family Membership Dues	$72	$ 60	$ 60	$40	$ 59
Single Membership Due	$54	$ 40	$ 40	$34	$ 39
Total Tennis Courts	27	19	11	6	10
Lighted Tennis Courts	12	7	7	4	10
Indoor/Bubble Courts	0	3	0	0	0
Racquetball Courts	6	2	8	0	7
Squash Courts	2	0	0	0	0
Swimming Pool	Y	Y	Y	N	N
Jacuzzi	Y	Y	Y	Y	N
Nautilus/Weight Center	Y	Y	Y	N	N
Aerobics/Dance Center	Y	Y	Y	Y	N
Pro Shop	Y	Y	Y	Y	N
Men & Women Steam Room	Y	N	N	N	N
Men & Women Sauna Room	Y	Y	Y	Y	N
Adult Lounge	Y	Y	Y	Y	Y
Cafe/Snack Bar	Y	Y	Y	Y	Y
Jr. Locker Room	Y	N	N	N	N
Jr. Lounge	Y	N	Y	N	N
Childcare	Y	Y	Y	Y	N
Office & Reception Area	Y	Y	Y	Y	Y
Tanning Booths	Y	Y	Y	N	N
Number Active Membership	150	680	665	150	1325
Potential Memberships	1,600	630	665	200	1325

improvements are not an optimum use but do contribute to the total property value over and above the value of the land only. Because of the specialized nature of recreational clubs, appraisers often have difficulties with highest and best use analysis.

Analyses of highest and best use should incorporate considerations of regional economic data, neighborhood factors, physical characteristics, legal constraints, and market conditions.

Regional data influencing commercial recreational clubs are primarily focused on the overall health of the area's economy. In general, more demand for recreational facilities is found in regions with strong, diversified economies, where there are populations with relatively high disposable incomes and reasonable amounts of leisure time. Considerations of climate also are appropriate in this analysis if the subject or its competition utilizes outdoor facilities.

Development patterns in the neighborhood surrounding a site may strongly influence its highest and best use. Appraisers should identify development heights and densities, complementary commercial uses, and concentrations of potential members in both residential and employment centers.

The physical characteristics of sites used for health and fitness clubs vary considerably, based primarily on the size of the facility and the land area that is necessary. Although small and irregularly shaped sites have been developed for health clubs, sites acceptable for health club developments do not limit other types of development. In general, most club sites are large, enjoy good access, and have necessary site improvements.

A site's development potential is largely influenced by its existing zoning, the potential of rezoning, and the orientation of surrounding development. Many recreational clubs are developed on sites zoned for commercial uses. An important consideration is that some urban areas will permit greater densities, or floor area ratios, than are necessary for most clubs. This consideration may result in a highest and best use that is more intensive than a recreational club because land value is too expensive. Another zoning consideration that could influence this analysis is parking requirements.

The feasibility of a club for the subject site is assessed in the market analysis section of the appraisal. This analysis should conclude that sufficient demand is available for the recreational facility in order to identify the club as the highest and best use. Market considerations for other uses also should be analyzed if other uses are physically possible and legally allowable. General market information can be obtained from regional economic trends and discussions with city officials, developers, brokers, and other appraisers familiar with a locality.

From this discussion, it is evident that the highest and best use analysis combines all aspects of influences on value. In assessing this determination, two points stand out. First, because the market for health clubs tends to be volatile, initial usage as a club may have to be changed. Thus, flexibility of the design and convertibility to other uses are positive influences. This consideration also may favorably influence potential lenders, as was evident from the survey results summarized in Chapter 6.

Second, although an analysis may conclude that a recreational club is the highest use, current operations may reveal a loss or only marginal profitability. In these cases, the appraiser should direct attention to the management of club operations. Inadequate or incompetent management may drag down a facility while analyses of the market, site, neighborhood, and existing improvements would indicate potential profitability if the services and programs are reoriented.

Site Valuation

The appraiser virtually always uses a sales comparison approach to estimate the market value of the subject site. Initially, recent sales and listings of vacant land considered somewhat comparable to the subject in terms of location, zoning, and proposed construction are identified. Adjustments are made if needed for date of sale, location, terms of sale and physical characteristics. These adjustments are most often made on a price per buildable unit or per square foot of land basis.

Many single-purpose commercial recreational clubs, except outdoor tennis clubs and health spas with overnight guests, are developed on commercially zoned land. In many cases, this land value is similar to that of vacant land used for neighborhood shopping centers or other medium-sized retail uses. This conclusion, however, depends primarily on the site's zoning and location. Some clubs are developed in light industrial or residential zones, depending on the restrictions imposed by the locality. Planned unit developments (PUDs) also may incorporate health clubs into a mixed-use setting. Health spas with overnight accommodations usually are built in zoning districts that permit hotel uses.

Site valuations are influenced to a large extent by the highest and best use of the land. In other words, if several uses are allowable on a site, the land value will be bid to its upper limit by the most profitable use. This consideration is particularly important when an existing recreational club does not represent the highest and best use if vacant but contributes sufficient interim value to make it the highest and best use as improved. These cases indicate a likelihood of substantial functional obsolescence in the cost approach.

When searching for comparable land sale data, the appraiser should seek information about vacant land sales purchased for development of similar commercial recreational clubs. However, because only a few, if any, of these sales are likely to have occurred, the appraiser then identifies other similarly zoned and located land sales. When adjusting these sales to the subject, the appraiser should consider differences in floor area ratio, zoning approvals, and use restrictions. For example, though the subject site and comparable may be similarly zoned, the subject may have a lesser parking requirement, resulting from its location in a mixed-use project or its proximity to transit. If these characteristics resulted in more buildable interior floor area on a site, the appraiser may want to upwardly adjust the comparable in relation to the subject.

Cost Approach

The cost approach is based on the assumption that an informed purchaser will pay no more for a property than the cost of producing a substitute property with the same utility. In the cost approach, the total value is computed as the addition of the market value of the land to the direct and indirect replacement costs of the improvements plus entrepreneurial profit less any depreciation from all causes. Land value is taken from the site valuation section of the appraisal. Sources for improvement replacement costs include:

- cost bids or reported actual construction costs of the subject;
- actual costs of recently constructed comparable properties;
- local contractors' opinions; and
- cost service data bases or manuals.

Entrepreneurial profit, necessary to motivate the development of real estate, is estimated from the time, money, and risk expended in bringing the property to an income-producing stage. In estimating any accrued depreciation, the appraiser considers such factors as age, condition, functional utility and detrimental external factors. The sum total of land costs, direct improvement costs, indirect costs, and entrepreneurial profit is the estimated replacement cost, new. Subtracting any required depreciation gives the value by the cost approach.

The cost approach is most applicable to new or proposed properties because few, if any, subjective adjustments of depreciation are usually needed. Although buyers of real estate rarely rely on the cost approach, appraisers use this approach to check the value attained by the income and sales comparison approaches. The cost approach is important to lenders because it generally establishes an upper limit for loan to value ratios.

The appraiser must analyze the reasonableness and accuracy of any cost estimate provided to him or her. This conclusion is reached, first, through discussions with the cost estimator, along with an assessment of the estimator's experience and knowledge of fitness club projects. Next, the appraiser can compare incurred or estimated subject construction costs to those for comparable recreational facilities. Finally, the appraiser can use a published cost service to verify the accuracy of a cost estimate or to roughly approximate construction costs from scratch.

The most commonly used cost service is the *Marshall Valuation Service* (MVS), published by Marshall and Swift. With the MVS an appraiser can estimate the present replacement cost of improvements through a calculator method (total average square footages by building type), a segregated cost method (accumulating average square footages by building component), or cost indicies and multiples (historical costs converted to present-day costs). The first two can be accomplished by manual computation or computer printout through telephone modem access.

Under the calculator method, the MVS identifies the following health- and fitness-related building types:

Building Type	Features
Health Clubs (Section 11)	Varied exercise areas; better clubs have snack bar, steam and sauna areas, and locker and shower rooms. Does not include whirlpools, swimming pools, or sports courts.
Handball/Racquetball Clubs (Section 16)	Basic playing courts, gym, sauna, snack bar, lockers and showers. Does not include spa facilities or furniture, fixtures and equipment (FF&E), such as lockers.
Indoor Tennis Clubs (Section 11)	Basic playing surfaces and ancillary facilities similar to handball/racquetball clubs.

The MVS does not include a separate category for health spas. For spas, the calculator method can be applied for hotels (Section 11) and modified for the types of facilities present. These adjustments for the types of facilities usually are derived from the "Segregated Cost Method." Other adjustments for facilities are obtainable from the "Supplemental Costs" section. Examples include swimming pools, parking lots, and landscaping (all from Section 66) and enclosures for sports courts and swimming pools (Section 67). Another cost category, which the manual does not include, includes furniture, fixtures, and equipment (FF&E) for clubs. Appraisers should add costs of office furnishings, lounge furniture, exercise equipment, and lockers separately. Trade journals and local distributors are good sources of costs for specialized exercise equipment.

To calculate a replacement cost new for the subject, the appraiser also must consider soft costs that are not included in the MVS. These include premarketing costs, loan fees (points), and entrepreneurial profit.

Table 8.2 provides a summary of a cost approach for a proposed tennis club.

Table 8.2 Example of Cost Approach Calculations for a New Tennis Club Using the Calculator Method

Construction Component	Unit Cost		Total Component Cost
Clubhouse: 21,592 Sq. Ft.	@ $60.00	=	$1,295,520
Tennis Courts: 27	@ $30,000	=	$ 810,000
(Includes fencing and lights)			
Swimming Pool:			
75′ × 28′ = 2,100 Sq. Ft.	@ $35.00	=	$ 73,500
Drives and Walkways:			
175,000 Sq. Ft.	@ 1.70	=	$ 297,500
Subtotal:			$2,476,520
Land Value: 14.9 Acres	@ $50,000/acre		$ 745,000
Total Hard Costs			$3,221,520
Soft Costs:			
Loan Fees: 2.5% of $3,000,000		$75,000	
Premarketing Expenses		$100,000	
Operational Overhead @ 5%		$161,076	
Total Indirect Costs			$ 336,076
Total Construction and Land Costs			$3,557,596
Plus Entrepreneurial Profit @ 10%			$ 355,760
Total Real Estate Costs			$3,913,356
Add F.F.&E.			$ 250,000
Indicated Value, Cost Approach, Including F.F.&E.			$4,163,356
		Rounded to:	$4,160,000

Sales Comparison Approach

This approach is based on the assumption that an informed buyer will pay no more for a property than the cost of acquiring an existing property with the same utility. The techniques employed involve comparing the subject property to recent sales or listings of similar recreational clubs located in comparable areas. The reliability of a value estimated from this approach depends on:

- the degree of comparability between the subject and sale comparables;
- the length of time since the sales were consummated;
- the verifiability and accuracy of the sales data; and
- the absence of unusual conditions affecting the comparable sale.

Unfortunately, appraisers typically are able to identify few transactions involving recreational clubs. This difficulty results because relatively few projects exist, many of the facilities now existing are new or nearly new, and most successful clubs have not been placed on the market. Many sales that have occurred have been conducted as a part of bankruptcy or foreclosure proceedings or under duress, making comparability to the subject even more difficult to quantify. Generally, because of the paucity of good data, value estimates for fitness clubs using the sales comparison approach are usually given little weight in a final reconciliation of value.

Sales of commercial recreational clubs usually are expressed in terms of price per square foot, price per court, or price per member. Other indices could include gross revenue multipliers or going-in capitalization rates. Where sales of somewhat comparable facilities are located, typical adjustments would include differences in date of sale, terms of sale, age, location, facilities, amenities, and membership. Appraisers also should discern if the sales include FF&E and the business value, if any, associated with the transaction. Each comparable sale is likely to require significant adjustments to provide comparability to the subject. Because of the differences, the appraiser may have difficulty attaining a precise estimate of value. Instead, the adjusted comparable sales may indicate a range within which the final value determination should fall.

If a subject includes a combination of facilities (i.e., outdoor tennis courts with a large separate health club on one site), separate sales comparison approaches may be advisable. The applicability of analyzing separate markets will depend on the availability of supporting sale data. This technique would work in the above example if sufficient sales data of outdoor tennis clubs with limited indoor facilities and multisport clubs were available. Value estimates for each category of activity are then added together to arrive at a total value estimate for the subject.

To become aware of those few sales or listings occurring in the illiquid recreational club market, the appraiser should work to develop contacts with developers, lenders, brokers, and other appraisers experienced in the industry. These parties usually are first to know when sales do occur.

An example of a market sales adjustment grid is illustrated in Table 8.3.

Table 8.3 Example of a Market Sales Adjustment Grid

Comparable Sale	1	2	3	4
Memberships:	750	1,134	720	278
Property Size:				
Courts	14	28	10	7
Square Feet	18,000	39,000*	14,000	8,600
Sale Price	$1,325,000	$7,100,000	$1,200,000	$650,000
Financing Terms	Normal	(100,000)	Normal	(110,000)
Leasehold Interest	+ 75,000	0	0	0
Excess Land	0	0	(200,000)	0
Normal Sale Price	$1,400,000	$7,000,000	$1,000,000	$540,000
Time (0.4%/Mo.)	+ 68,000	+ 168,000	+ 101,000	+ 40,500
Location	0	(700,000)	0	+ 54,000
Physical Char.	0	(2,200,000)	0	0
Adjusted Sales Price	$1,468,600	$4,268,000	$1,101,000	$634,500
Price Per Court	$ 104,900	$ 152,429	$ 110,100	$ 90,643
Price Per Square Foot	$ 81.59	$ 109.43	$ 78.64	$ 73.78
Price Per Membership	$ 1,958	$ 3,764	$ 1,529	$ 2,282
GRM	2.65	3.38	2.35	4.50

* Excludes 22 hotel rooms.

Income Approach

This approach is based on the economic principle that the value of a property capable of producing income is the present worth of anticipated future benefits. The annual cash flow or net income projection is converted into a present value indication using a discounting and/or capitalization process. Methods of capitalization are based on inherent assumptions concerning the quality, durability, and pattern of the income stream.

The direct capitalization method is based on application of an overall capitalization rate to a single year's net operating income. This technique is appropriate for an existing property where the current income is equal or close to the stabilized fair market rate.

Where the pattern of projected income is either irregular during the absorption period or simply has not stabilized, discounted cash flow analysis (yield capitalization) is most appropriate. This method is based on the present worth of future cash flow expectancies calculated by individually discounting each anticipated collection at an appropriate discount rate. The market value attained through this approach is the accumulation of the present worth of each year's projected net income plus the present worth of the terminal value or reversion. The estimated value of the reversion, that is, the forecasted property value at the end of the projection period, can be based on a projected appreciation or depreciation of the project value or on a direct capitalization of the reversion year's projected net income.

The income approach usually produces the most reliable value estimate for most types of recreational clubs because it most accurately mirrors how investors arrive at price decisions. In most cases, clubs are analyzed as ongoing income-producing businesses or enterprises. The income approach consists of five basic steps:

- selecting the appropriate projection period;
- estimating potential gross income;
- forecasting annual expenses;
- selecting appropriate discount and capitalization rates; and
- applying the proper discounting and capitalization procedures.

Projection Period

Projection periods generally range from one to ten years. The period should extend to the time when the property's net income stream becomes stabilized, which occurs when both occupancy at market levels and expenses become relatively constant or established.

One-year projection periods are appropriate for existing properties that have reached a point of stabilized membership and expenses. Direct capitalization is applied to the stabilized net income to arrive at an estimate of value from the income approach.

More typical projection periods range from two to five years, which reflect normal absorption periods for recreational clubs. For example, if a development has a 24-month absorption period measured from the completion of construction, the projection period would be 36 months. This premise is based on the owner of the property receiving the cash flow benefits (deficits) during the two-year absorption period and the net proceeds of a hypothetical sale (reversion value) at the end of the second year, based on the projected and stabilized third year's net income. The value of the reversion at the end of the 24-month period is based on a direct capitalization of the third year's net income. The theory is that the investor purchasing the property at the end of the second year would be more interested in the anticipated net income in the first year of ownership than the previous year's net income under prior ownership. The cash flow of the project's first two years and the value of the reversion are converted to present value through the use of an appropriate discount rate.

Many lenders and developers prefer a traditional ten-year projection period analysis for a sophisticated income-producing property. The appraiser conducts the same calculations described above, discounting the annual cash flows for the first ten years of the projection and discounting the value of the reversion, which is the direct capitalization of the projected eleventh-year income.

Long projection periods are rarely utilized in analyses of recreational clubs. However they may be necessary if a property is subject to a sublease or ground lease that was due to expire or provides for changing rent levels within the foreseeable future. The ultimate use of the appraisal, particularly where the payment of debt service is critical, could influence the decision to employ a longer analysis period.

Projecting absorption periods and membership patterns for recreational clubs is difficult and imprecise. Recent operating histories of comparable facilities may inaccurately indicate absorption merely because of demographics. In estimating the absorption period, the appraiser should consider:

- the number of memberships to be absorbed;
- the actual memberships, potential memberships, and any waiting lists at comparable facilities;
- the subject's position in its competitive environment and its competitive advantages/deficiencies;
- results of the market penetration analysis;
- results of primary market research;
- recreational development experience of the developers; and
- depth of the marketing campaign.

An appraiser will usually assume an even absorption pattern during the absorption period. However, actual market experience shows that absorption is not even; a higher percentage of memberships sell during the early months of the project with the remaining memberships stretching out the absorption period. Forecasting a noneven absorption pattern is often more difficult to support than a conservative estimate of an equal or regular absorption pattern.

Potential Gross Income

Potential gross income is the maximum rent or revenue that a facility can achieve, given its competitive market position. Market rent or fees are drawn from the analysis of existing and proposed comparable projects in the market feasibility study. The appraiser can summarize the results of this survey in a grid using a range, average, and most comparable fees for initiation, dues, and usage costs.

The appraiser should objectively evaluate the subject's competitive advantages and disadvantages when estimating market rents. This evaluation can only be accomplished through an exhaustive review of similar property types. Appraisers quantify the comparison of the subject to other projects using an adjustment grid, adjusting each in relation to the subject. The appraiser can adjust for age, location, construction quality, facilities and amenities. After all adjustments have been made, the comparables should theoretically reflect an approximate market fee structure or revenue base for the subject.

Other Considerations

Conclusions reached in a survey of competitive properties are supported by the results of primary market research. These studies can provide direct market evidence supporting proposed, existing, or more appropriate membership fees; other charges; and rent levels for the subject.

Sometimes, a proposed project, particularly a high-end recreational club or health spa resort, will not be directly comparable to any existing facilities within the primary market area. Although common sense suggests that a higher quality facility can command higher levels of income, this differential often is difficult to quantify. Above-market proposed fees must be linked to market evidence. Appraisers facing this challenge will need to examine comparables outside the primary market area in locations with similar demographics and economics to find market support for higher quality properties. Though these facilities do not compete directly with the subject, they provide evidence for market acceptance of higher rents in exchange for higher quality/greater amenities.

For clubs that charge relatively high initial membership fees, the appraiser must project a probability of turnover. Surveys indicate that a high percentage of fitness clubs' members do not use the facilities regularly within three months of joining. Thus, clubs are able to sell more memberships without adversely affecting capacity usage of facilities. Some clubs, such as exclusive country clubs, have more rigidly fixed membership levels and projected turnover rates for these types of clubs generally are low. For an existing club, the percentage of membership turnover usually is derived from historical club operating data. In the case of proposed clubs, the appraiser must utilize a figure obtained through an investigation of comparables in the local market. According to IRSA, attrition rates for members range from a low of 14.5% for tennis clubs to 39.8% for multirecreation clubs without pools. Attrition and net growth rates for the industry are summarized in Table 8.4. These figures can be compared with the subject operations to gauge its operational performance. Net growth rates, and attrition rates for fully-occupied clubs, are necessary for calculating initiation and annual membership fees.

Table 8.4 Annual Membership Changes by Club Types

Club Type	Growth Rates*		Attrition Rates	
	Memberships	Members	Memberships	Members
Tennis				
Average Club	6.3%	7.6%	15.4%	14.5%
Top 5	(0.6)%	(1.0)%	27.6%	27.5%
R-ball/Squash				
Average Club	27.8%	31.5%	37.2%	33.9%
Top 5	11.5%	20.7%	36.3%	38.6%
Fitness				
Average Club	29.4%	31.3%	27.9%	26.2%
Top 5	N/A	N/A	N/A	N/A
Multisport w/o Pool				
Average Club	6.5%	7.5%	29.8%	26.5%
Top 5	0.0%	0.5%	39.4%	39.8%
Multisport w/Pool				
Average Club	7.0%	7.7%	35.3%	33.4%
Top 5	(0.9)%	(0.7)%	19.7%	19.8%

* Growth rates reflect net increases (or decreases) in membership after adding new members and subtracting attritions. Attrition rates reflect the gross number dropped during the year divided by total members or memberships.

Source: IRSA, "Profiles of Success—1987 State of the Industry Report," 1987, pp. 31-32.

Departmental Income

Most recreational clubs will generate revenue from several other categories in addition to membership entry fees, recurring charges, and usage fees. To a large extent, the types and amounts of this income will depend on the club's membership level and the types of facilities and amenities the club includes. Examples of these revenue sources include food and beverage, pro shop, instruction classes and vending machines. These revenue categories were discussed in Chapter 7 and presented in Tables 7.11 and 7.12. In the income approach, the information compiled in the market study is utilized for forecasting these revenues. Data sources include historical club operating statements, operating information from competitive clubs in the market area, and industry averages.

Food and beverage income can comprise a major portion of a club's revenues. As shown in Table 7.11, the average multisport club obtained over 10% of its revenues from food and beverage operations. Food and beverage revenues usually are based on the floor area, number of seats, or projected covers. Certain clubs contain a separate facility that is open to the public and functions more as a restaurant than a food and beverage component of a health club. In these cases, appraisers are advised to consult Stephen Rushmore's book *Hotels, Motels, and Restaurants—Valuations and Market Studies*, published by the American Institute of Real Estate Appraisers.

Underutilization and Collection Losses

A general fixture for a vacancy factor is usually not deducted from all revenue sources to arrive at an estimate of effective gross income in analyses of commercial recreational clubs. Rather, deductions for absorption period revenue loss and an allowance for the normal turnover of memberships after stabilization are provided in the membership revenue projections. Thus, an additional deduction for underutilization loss would represent a double-counting of this item. In most market areas, appraisers should not use the maximum potential club membership as a basis for projecting revenues. Using a membership figure below the maximum level incorporates a function similar to a vacancy and collection loss used in income approach analyses for other property types. This technique would not be appropriate for a rental property, which should be analyzed in a manner similar to retail properties. In some cases, appraisers may apply a small percentage for rent collection delinquencies or delays.

Operating Expenses

Operating expenses are the periodic expenditures necessary to maintain the subject and to continue the production of effective gross income. Operating expenses are estimated on a cash basis and do not include capital expenditures, one-time expenditures, expenses unique to a particular management, debt service, depreciation, or income taxes.

Operating expenses consist of three components: (1) fixed expenses; (2) variable expenses; and (3) reserves for replacements. Fixed expenses are operating expenses that generally do not vary with occupancy and are incurred whether a project is full or vacant. Variable expenses include all expenditures that vary with occupancy or the intensity of property operation. Both of these expense categories were discussed in Chapter 7. Replacement reserves are allocations providing for the periodic replacement of building and equipment components that wear out more rapidly than the building itself.

The annual reserve allocation is estimated from the cost of replacement prorated over the remaining life of the building component. These components can include roof areas, carpeting, all furniture and equipment, and landscaping. This reserve is a cost component that is used by appraisers for the proper valuation of real property. Reserves for replacements usually are not found in operating statements prepared by accountants for other purposes.

After estimating all expenses on a line-by-line basis, the appraiser should examine the estimate of total expenses relative to the size of the development and percentage of effective gross income. The appraiser should use his or her judgment, experience, and knowledge of comparable recreational clubs to evaluate the reasonableness of the total operating expenses. Industry averages also should be compared to the projected ratios for the subject. These averages for the industry, as published by IRSA for 1987, are illustrated in Table 8.5.

Table 8.5   Operating Expense Ratios

| | Average Club Size | | Expenses | | |
Club Type	Sq. Ft.	Members	% of EGI	Per Sq. Ft.	Per Member
Tennis					
Average Club	47,522	1,298	74.4%	$ 9.53	$349
Top 5	—	1,007	58.0%	—	$312
R-ball/Squash					
Average Club	22,253	1,568	69.2%	$19.17	$272
Top 5	—	1,718	52.3%	—	$185
Fitness					
Average Club	15,411	1,870	68.7%	$28.58	$236
Top 5	—	N/A	N/A	—	N/A
Multisport w/o Pool					
Average Club	52,106	2,287	70.4%	$15.40	$351
Top 5	—	1,898	51.3%	—	$361
Multisport w/Pool					
Average Club	69,340	3,215	69.1%	$17.11	$369
Top 5	—	2,856	50.8%	—	$290

Source: IRSA, "Profiles of Success—1987 State of the Industry Report", 1987.

This figure illustrates that the ranges for operating expenses by club type are rather narrow. For example, the highest ratio of operating expenses to effective gross income was 74.4% for average tennis clubs and the lowest percentage was 69.2% for fitness clubs. On a per member and per square foot basis, the unit expense ranges were broader. These ranges are dependent on a club's total development size, physical features, services, rent level, and location. As discussed previously, appraisers should exercise caution when applying these industry averages. Priority should be placed on local operating data derived from the market.

Capitalization Rates

A capitalization rate is a factor that represents the relationship between one year's net income and value. The rate is expressed as a decimal factor divided into the net income to realize an estimate of value by the income approach.

$$\text{Value} = \frac{\text{Net operating income}}{\text{Capitalization rate}}$$

The components of the capitalization rate provide for a return on capital (operating capital, real estate, and personal property), recapture of investment in depreciable assets, and an allowance for management or return to the entrepreneur. The latter factor represents the business portion of the capitalization rate. These requirements result in rates that are higher for recreational clubs compared with typical commercial real estate projects such as offices, apartments, or shopping centers.

The real estate aspects of a club may be separated from the business enterprise where a lease for the facilities is involved. Under this condition, a lower capitalization rate would be applicable for the appraisal of the owner's or leased fee interest, and a higher rate would be appropriate for the entrepreneurial aspect or leasehold interest. In theory, the summation of the proper weighing of these two rates would result in the same capitalization rate applied to the net income where no lease existed.

Ideally, capitalization rates should be derived from the market, that is, from the sales of comparable clubs. The nature of this analysis in practice generally is difficult because few sales of commercial recreational clubs meet the test of comparability. To derive an accurate capitalization rate from market data, the appraiser must have a complete understanding of the transaction. This investigation requires the cooperation of the buyer and seller to verify both the terms of the sale and their motivations. Special factors to consider when deriving rates from the market include the effect of financing terms on value; market conditions as they affect competition and income-producing potential; special motivational factors, such as a tax shelter or a property trade; and property conditions, such as deferred maintenance.

Where buyers and sellers feel that proprietary information should remain confidential, the appraiser's research assignment becomes extremely difficult. Because of this general lack of reliable market data and the relative availability of club financing information, capitalization rates commonly are derived by a method known as band-of-investment theory. This technique combines the weighted average of the return required by the mortgage portion of the investment with the return or dividend requirement of the equity portion. This latter component commonly is expressed as cash on cash return or spendable income rate. Appraisers also refer to this term as the equity dividend rate.

The premise of the band-of-investment technique is the assumption that most properties are purchased with debt and equity capital and that each investment position requires a market-determined return on investment. These rates include a competitive interest rate to the debt holder (the lender) and a competitive equity yield to the equity investor (the developer or owner). Band-of-investment calculations are illustrated as follows:

Component	Ratio	Rate	Rate Component
Mortgage:	Loan to value ratio	× Mortgage constant	= Weighted average of debt
Equity:	Equity to value ratio	× Equity dividend rate	= Weighted average of equity
			+
Total			Overall capitalization rate

Typically, loan-to-value ratios of 60% or more make capitalization rates very sensitive to mortgage conditions.

Although mortgage terms are readily available, it is often a difficult and imprecise process to estimate the equity dividend rate that reflects the higher risks involved in commercial recreational clubs. Sources that are likely to be helpful to the appraiser include developers, brokers, and lenders familiar with clubs. These parties are often aware of capitalization rate ranges for various types of clubs. The appraiser must then assess the advantages, disadvantages, and risks inherent in the subject property itself to estimate properly the subject's likely capitalization rate within the range.

Appraisers generally have utilized capitalizations rates from a low of 10% (existing profitable clubs) to a high of 15% (proposed clubs). These rates are similar to those used in the capitalization analysis of hotel/motel investments because they also are real estate oriented businesses that require the application of unique managerial skills and exhibit special risk considerations.

Discount Rates

Discount rates are factors applied to annual net operating cash flows and to the property's future or reversion value to arrive at an estimate of net present value using a discounted cash flow technique. They are comprised of the annual cash-on-cash return (equity dividend rate) less an estimate of the property's yearly appreciation rate plus the annual inflation rate. Discount rates for recreational clubs also are influenced by investors' expectations in this market. In our experience, discount rates will approximate 12% to 16%, depending on the quality of the subject's estimated income stream, the forecasted length of the absorption period, and the degree of investment risk.

Reconciliation of Values

The last step in the appraisal process is the final reconciliation of value. Estimating a value involves a weighing process; it is applied to the individual approaches and considers the strength of their substantiation by market and other sources of data. Appraisers also must weigh the reliability and applicability of particular approaches as they affect recreational properties. The development of a final estimate of value involves judgment in a careful and logical analysis of the procedures leading to each indication of value. The judgment criteria include appropriateness, accuracy, and quantity of evidence.

The chief benefit of the cost approach lies in the fact that it shows actual replacement cost combined with the current fair market value of the land. It can provide insight into the overall feasibility of a project; for example, where it indicates a value substantially greater than those of the other two approaches, one could conclude that the improvements did not represent the highest and best use of the site. This consideration is particularly important when appraising proposed developments. The primary weakness of this approach is that it fails to consider the dynamics of the real estate investment market. The cost approach also does not provide any estimate of business value attached to a property or enterprise, except by franchise prices, which are rare.

The income approach generally is considered to be the best and most accurate measure of value for income-producing properties. This approach most closely duplicates the process used by a well-informed investor and best illustrates the income potential of the property. The income approach is appropriate for new developments because it factors in costs of absorption and the discounting to the present value. The income approach deals with projected income and expenses for the subject and reflects market activity through the capitalization process. The appraiser should consider that the income approach analysis for operating commercial recreational facilities usually includes an allowance for the business value of the enterprise in addition to the value of the real estate.

The sales comparison approach is considered a reliable approach when sales data are available that are sufficiently similar to the subject property to allow a meaningful comparison. In most cases, sales require adjustments for location, physical characteristics, date of sale, terms of sale, and a consideration of existing leases. Primarily because of dissimilar physical characteristics and locations of comparables, subjective judgments must be made. Therefore, a lower degree of emphasis is placed on this approach unless comparables that require limited adjustments are available.

After the approaches have been carefully reviewed and weighted and a value conclusion for the entire property has been estimated, it is frequently necessary to allocate the total value among the investment components. For example, the appraisal of the fee simple interest can be allocated among the land, site improvements, buildings, personal property (FF&E), and the business or goodwill. Physical assets typically are allocated on the basis of the cost approach. The contribution of the business value or goodwill may be estimated using more than one technique.

Business Valuation

Two typical situations involve appraisals of clubs: (1) the club operates in leased quarters, and (2) the club owns the real estate and other assets. Leased quarters can be in a multiple tenancy or in a freestanding building. Analyses of contributions of intangible factors to the overall value follow the same methodologies in all cases.

As a simplification, the business value may be estimated as the difference between the income approach and the cost approach. (In this equation, the cost approach can be substituted for a reconciled value of the real estate between the cost and sales comparison approaches if the value indicated by the sales comparison approach includes only the real estate.) In appraisal terminology, the business value also is known as goodwill. The goodwill includes the ability to retain old and attract new patronage plus intangible assets, such as franchises and licenses, which aid the facility's reputation and income-producing potential.

Another method to separate the business value from the overall enterprise is to differentiate appropriate cash flows and capitalization rates. Application of this technique requires strong market sales data of leased and fee simple interests for similar operating clubs. Theoretically, appropriate segments of the net operating income are attributable to the physical and intangible assets. In practice, limited market data usually prevent the application of this technique.

The appraiser must keep the concepts of real estate valuation and business valuation separate in order to determine an appropriate value. While it is difficult to separate income streams attributable to the real estate and the business, the reconciliation of the approaches should indicate if a difference exists. In many cases, goodwill or business value is not present, and the reconciled value represents the real estate alone.

Case Studies

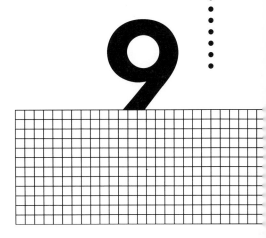

The focus of this chapter is to provide a brief survey of the facility types an appraiser may encounter. The examples are not intended to be comprehensive in scope. There are too many permutations of club facilities and services to provide case studies of all of the types of operations we have attempted to address in this book. Rather, these case studies illustrate some of the techniques outlined in this book and some of the physical, operational, and analytical problems in the market.

Data compiled from each club varied in terms of detail, quantity, and reporting period. We have attempted to derive as much operating information as possible from each case. Thus, far more data and analysis are provided for some clubs than for others.

General descriptive data are provided to preserve the confidentiality of the cases. These cases provide various formats of income and expense data, which dramatize the need for standardization in the industry. Complete market feasibility analyses and appraisals are not furnished in this chapter because of space limitations. Furthermore, generalizations about income, expenses, capitalization rates, and so forth, should not be extrapolated from these examples. Each fitness facility must be evaluated individually; appraisers should utilize actual operations' history of the subject and competitors, evaluate future competition and trends, and determine appropriate local market characteristics.

Case A: Proposed Tennis Club

This primarily outdoor tennis club is a proposed project that is part of a 500-acre planned development located in a suburban area of the western United States. Population in this community is projected to grow 15% in 5 years. Eight competitive facilities are located within 12 miles of the subject, and all but one of these are operating near full capacity.

Land Area:	14.9 acres
Building Area:	21,600 square feet
Courts:	27 outdoor tennis courts (12 lighted)
	6 racquetball courts
	2 squash courts
Other Facilities:	Six-lane, 25-meter outdoor heated swimming pool; children's outdoor wading pool; separate men's and women's locker rooms including jacuzzis, steam room, saunas and tanning booths; child care; pro shop; weight rooms; aerobics rooms; lounge and cafe/snack bar
Age:	New
Size of Membership:	Current pre-opening sales—150
	Potential—1,600
Membership Fees:	Initiation—none
	Family monthly dues—$72.00
	Single monthly dues—$54.00

Projected Operating Results

Within a 6-mile radius of the subject, the existing population was estimated at 145,000. The three competitors also within this area yielded 48,333 persons per competitor. This penetration figure is 52% greater than the benchmark market penetration of 31,772 persons per competitor within 5.9 miles provided by IRSA. The addition of the subject club would drop the number of persons per competitor to 36,250, which is 14% above the benchmark figure. Other demographic indicators provided additional market support for this facility. No other proposed competitors were known or planned in the market area.

The appraiser concluded that an initiation fee was not appropriate during the absorption period. For the stabilized year, a $200 initiation fee was projected and a 10% annual turnover.

After investigating the performance of other recently completed tennis clubs in the market area and the market feasibility study, the appraiser estimated 50% absorption as of completion of construction. At a pace of 80 new memberships per quarter, stabilized occupancy was estimated at 24 months based on a membership level of 1,280 (80% of capacity members).

Analysis of operating data from local competitors and national surveys resulted in an overall operating expense ratio of 51.5%. An analysis of operating expenses follows.

Breakdown of Expense Categories

According to IRSA, expenses are divided into the following categories:

1. Operating expenses;
2. Direct expenses;
3. Cost of goods sold; and
4. Indirect expenses and fixed expenses.

In addition to these expenses, an additional category of expenses that represents real operating costs are management and reserve expenses. Although these expenses were not covered in the IRSA survey, they are included for valuation purposes.

Direct and operating expenses are broken down into the following categories:

- payroll;
- payroll related expenses;
- advertising and promotion;
- commissions;
- contract services;
- equipment;
- licenses;
- dues;
- subscriptions;
- printing and stationery;
- refreshments;
- repairs and maintenance;
- supplies;
- uniforms;

- travel; and

- other expenses.

Cost of goods is included for pro shop sales and food and beverage sales. These expenses ranged from 12.1% to 20.8% of total income generated from these departments.

Indirect and fixed expenses include the following:

- general repairs and maintenance;

- energy;

- utilities;

- marketing and sales;

- general and administrative;

- real estate and personal property taxes;

- property and business insurance; and

- other expenses.

These expenses accounted for 38.7% to 48.3% of total income generated.

IRSA statistics indicate that total expenses account for 50.8% (top 5 clubs) to 69.1% (average club) of total income generated, or between $410.97 (of the top 5 clubs) to $594.26 (for the average clubs) per membership. These expenses result in net operating income ranging from 49.2% (for the top 5 clubs surveyed) to 30.9% (for average clubs in the survey) of total income, or between $398.03 (top 5 clubs) to $265.74 (average club) per membership per year.

In addition to these operating expenses, a management and reserve expense of 8% of gross operating income is deducted, for a total estimated expense of $587,238 or 51.49% of total income generated or $459 per potential membership per year.

Replacement reserves are necessary for items such as furniture, fixtures, equipment, carpeting, and other items of personal property. The appraiser estimated replacement/repair reserves at 3% of gross income. For management expense, in view of the critical nature of management and promotion, a 5% factor is applied of effective gross income.

Note: Expenses as shown are based on 1,280 active memberships (that is, 1,600 potential memberships × 80% × $387.50 = $496,000 + $91,238 [added expenses of management and reserves of 8% of GOI of $1,159,680 = $92,774] = $588,774).

Analysis of Net Operating Income

IRSA statistics indicate net operating income that ranges from 49.20% (top 5 clubs) to 30.90% (average club) of total income generated, or between $398.03 (top 5 clubs) to $265.74 (average club) per active membership per year. Two tennis clubs in the competitive market area reported net operating incomes, per active membership per year, of $315.42 to $365.63.

Capitalization Process

Because the projected net income represents a stabilized operating amount, the income is capitalized by application of a direct overall rate derived from both comparable sales as well as from other real estate capitalization data. Recreation complexes throughout California and other Western states have generally exhibited overall capitalization rates ranging from 10.5% to 15%. The sales comparison approach included two sales where rates could be extracted, which were 10.1% and 11.11%. However, these rates were given limited weight because the established operating data were erratic and complete verification of the figures was not possible.

More weight was given to rates derived from sales of special use properties that include business operations, such as hotels, nursing homes, convenience stores, and so forth. The overall rates from these types of on-going concern properties range between 10% to as high as 15%. Because of the risk associated with a proposed club and the high level of management involved with a sport facility, the appraiser concluded that an appropriate capitalization rate for the subject property was 15%.

The conclusion of the stabilized value by the income approach is illustrated in Table 9.1. The concluded stabilized value, assuming completion of the proposed improvements as planned, was $3,806,000.

Estimated Income Loss During Membership Buildup

For satisfying the appraisal reporting requirements of Memorandum 41-C (R-41C) of the Federal Home Bank Board, the projected loss of income during a membership buildup period from that projected assuming a stabilized level of operation, as of the date of completion of the facility, is analyzed and calculated. The stabilized level of 80% of the total potential membership was estimated to be achieved by the end of the eighth quarter following completion of the facility, or at a rate of 80

Table 9.1   Tennis Club Stabilized Value

1,600 potential members × 80% = 1,280 memberships
   75% family = 960 memberships
   25% single = 320 memberships

Gross Income

Membership Dues

Family: 960 × $72.00 × 12 = $829,440
Single: 320 × $54.00 × 12 = $207,360

Total Membership Dues	$1,036,800

Initiation Fees

1,280 × 10% × $150 =	19,200

Other Income

10% of Dues	103,680
Total Gross Income	$1,159,680

Less Expenses

Operations: 1,280 × $387.50 =	$ 496,000
Management & Reserves:	
8% of $1,159,680 =	$ 92,774
Total Expenses	$ 588,774
Net Income	$ 570,906
Capitalized at 15%	$3,806,040
Called,	$3,806,000

memberships per quarter, assuming a 50% pre-sale of memberships. The calculation of the estimated loss of profit during this period from what would be obtainable assuming a stabilized level of operation is outlined in Figure 9.2. The net income projected for each of the eight quarters of the absorption period is based on the following calculations:

Total membership capacity:		1,600
Estimated stabilized membership as a percent of capacity:		
(80)%	=	1,280
Estimated pre-sales as a percent of stabilized level:		
1,280 members × 50% pre-sales	=	640
Remaining memberships to be sold during absorption:		640
Membership sales per quarter during absorption period:		
640 memberships divided by 8 quarters	=	80/quarter or
		27 (R)/month

Because the estimated fixed expenses include commission expenses attributed to normal membership attrition rates only, additional commission expenses have been included to reflect a real or net growth of 80 memberships per quarter. These commission expenses are based on a 5.5% commission paid on one year's membership dues.

Table 9.2 Present Value of Income Loss During Absorption for a Proposed Tennis Club

Quarters	1	2	3	4	
Memberships	640	720	800	880	
Gross Income Per Membership Per Month	74.25	74.25	74.25	74.25	
Gross Income	142,560	160,380	178,200	196,020	
Operating Expenses	145,504	145,504	145,504	145,504	
Commissions	3,564	3,564	3,564	3,564	
Net Income	(6,508)	11,312	29,132	46,952	
Stabilized Net Income	138,311	138,311	138,311	138,311	
Future Value (loss)	(144,819)	(126,999)	(109,179)	(91,359)	
P.V. Factor @ 11%	0.9742	0.9492	0.9247	0.9009	
Present Value	(141,083)	(120,547)	(100,958)	(82,305)	
Quarters	**5**	**6**	**7**	**8**	**9**
Memberships	960	1,040	1,120	1,200	1,280
Rates Per Membership	74.25	74.25	74.25	74.25	74.25
Gross Income	213,840	231,660	249,480	267,300	285,120
Operating Expenses	145,504	145,504	145,504	145,504	147,194
Commissions	3,564	3,564	3,564	3,564	0
Net Income	64,772	82,592	100,412	118,232	137,926
Stabilized Net Income	138,311	138,311	138,311	138,311	138,311
Future Value (loss)	(73,539)	(55,719)	(37,899)	(20,079)	(385)
P.V. Factor @ 11%	0.8777	0.8551	0.8331	0.8116	0.7907
Present Value	(64,545)	(47,645)	(31,574)	(16,296)	(304)

Total Loss: $605,257; Say; $605,000

The resulting quarterly losses are discounted at 11%, which is considered a relatively safe rate to reflect the present value of income lost from what a stabilized operating level would generate during this same period. The total present value of these losses was calculated at $605,000, and the resulting discounted value was $3,806,000 minus $605,000 equals $3,201,000.

Case B: Successful Racquetball Club

This racquetball club is located in a growing suburban community of a major metropolitan area on the West Coast. Over 70% of local households have incomes greater than $25,000. No other racquetball facilities are present within the subject's city limits, but five other racquetball clubs are located within a nine-mile radius.

Land Area	1.58 acres
Building Area:	21,081 square feet
Courts:	11 racquetball courts
Other Facilities:	Fitness area, lounge, lockers and showers, pro shop, child care area, snack bar, separate men's and women's sauna, steam room and jacuzzi, sun deck and outdoor tennis/basketball court.
Age:	7 years
Size of Membership:	1,500 memberships 2,100 to 2,200 persons
Membership Fees:	Initiation Fees: Single—$300.00 Family—$375.00
Monthly dues:	Single—$54.00 Family—$84.00

Operating Results

Net operating income was $347,900 in 1986. Actual income/expense data are summarized in Table 9.3. Some operating expense categories were changed because of a new accounting system that was installed in 1985.

Table 9.3   Successful Racquetball Club Operating History

Income	1984	1985	1986
Initiation			
Corporate	$ 12,913	$ 9,083	$ 11,490
Reinstatement	986	4,547	4,976
Fitness	30,144	63,264	62,418
Racquetball	46,509	42,393	51,575
Total Initiation	$ 90,552	$ 119,287	$ 130,459
Dues			
Racquetball	$373,530	$ 400,399	415,590
Fitness	237,394	396,000	532,343
Summer	25,731	20,209	15,324
Other	650	1,823	841
Total Dues	$637,305	$ 818,431	$ 964,098
Total Initiation & Dues	$727,857	$ 937,718	$1,094,557
Other Income			
Racquetball	$ 86,339	$ 60,472	$ 63,042
Fitness	11,123	12,807	17,296
Food & Bev.	45,752	52,872	71,613
Towel	7,652	12,644	14,229
Tournament & League	16,053	12,748	11,212
Pro Shop	47,670	35,476	33,321
Tanning	2,721	4,969	4,080
Child Care	2,406	3,612	5,294
Other	7,447	12,894	18,649
Total	$227,183	$ 208,494	$ 238,736
Total Income	$955,040	$1,146,212	$1,333,293

Continued on next page

Expenses	1984	1985	1986
Purchases	$ 61,454	$ 52,293	$ 103,974
Advertising/Promo.	23,311	36,121	31,515
Acct./Computer/Office	9,949	1,551	26,084
Auto	897	1,444	1,325
Cash over/short	1,670	3,273	1,728
Dues/Subscriptions	1,199	1,206	2,516
Fitness	20,704	20,337	0
Insurance	7,427	9,299	2,422
Laundry	18,706	29,071	21,416
Maintenance & Repair	42,007	43,616	58,466
Management/Payroll	319,411	372,304	492,304
Employee Benefits	1,471	1,301	5,133
Supplies	43,588	55,663	47,726
Misc. & Licenses	544	1,893	27,984
Personal Prpty. Tax	1,680	4,456	3,943
Real Estate Tax	19,177	21,835	20,433
Racquetball	29,334	21,576	0
Telephone	6,492	10,378	11,316
Travel	1,090	1,275	3,604
Utilities	49,406	54,520	63,494
Land Rent	42,977	51,580	59,998
Total Operating Expenses	$706,896	$ 794,992	$ 985,381
Net Operating Income	$248,144	$ 351,220	$ 347,912
Overall Expense Ratio	74.0%	69.4%	73.9%
Expense Ratio Excluding Land Rent	69.5%	64.9%	69.4%

Analysis

This racquetball club is operating at typical market levels. Membership of this club (136 per court) is at or a little above 100% capacity, which could indicate a slightly reduced membership level if a new competitor enters the market. The fee and dues structure of this facility are at market and competitive with other nearby facilities. Operating expenses for this club, excluding property taxes and land rent, amount to about 68% of effective gross income, which is within the normal range for this type of facility. For example, IRSA reported operating expenses before fixed charges of 64% for the average racquetball/squash club in 1986.

In the appraisal of this club, a 5% risk and loss adjustment was made to the gross income to account for potential credit loss and possible loss of membership to a new competitor, even though no proposed projects were known. Property taxes were not included in operating expenses, and the appraiser added the property tax rate (1.08%) to the capitalization rate. In this jurisdiction, assessed value is 100% of the sale price, and the appraisal assumed a sale and reassessment of the subject.

The land lease had 73 years remaining, and the appraiser concluded that a direct capitalization approach was appropriate.

Stabilized net operating income		
(before land rent, property and personal taxes)		$375,000
Replacements for reserves		
(3% of EGI or $1,300,000)		$ 39,000
Income available for capitalization		$336,000
Capitalization rate:	12.00%	
Property tax rate:	1.08%	
Overall cap rate:	13.08%	

The net cash flow of $336,000 capitalized by an overall rate of 13.08% indicated a total leasehold value of $2,568,807 ($336,000 divided by .1308), rounded to $2,570,000.

The value by the income approach yielded equivalent values of $233,636 per racquetball court or $121.91 per square foot of building area. These units values, particularly the per court figure, were not supported by market sales. Although the value may appear high, it is supported by the economics of this operation. This upper-income community supports a relatively high fee structure. The value per square foot is comparable to sales of shopping centers without major anchors in this area.

The cost approach yielded a leasehold value of $2,300,000, which is 10.5% above the value by the income approach. The cost approach included an allocation of 15% for developer's overhead and profit, which the appraiser judged as reasonable. A 25% allocation for overhead and profit could have yielded a cost approach conclusion more consonant with the income approach conclusion. In this case, however, the appraiser attributed the difference (about $270,000) to the value of the intangibles associated with the business, such as goodwill.

Case C: Problem Racquetball Club

This racquetball club is located in a depressed midwestern suburban community of a major metropolitan area. The local economy, which is extremely dependent on heavy industry, is performing poorly; and the potential for substantial rejuvenation in the near future is minimal. Eight competitive facilities are located in the market area. The club with the best facilities, including an indoor swimming pool, six indoor tennis courts, a fitness club, a cocktail lounge and restaurant, is located two miles from the subject; and its monthly dues are $28.00 compared with

$27.00 for the subject. Thus, the upside revenue potential is considered slight.

Land area:	2.01 acres
Building area:	26,130 square feet
Courts:	12 racquetball courts
Other facilities:	Three former racquetball courts have been converted into a weight/fitness room and two aerobics rooms. Other facilities include a snack bar, separate men's and women's locker rooms and sauna, one jacuzzi, and pro shop.
Age:	Seven years
Size of membership:	940
Membership fees:	Initiation—$112.00 Monthly dues—$27.00

Operating Results

Net operating income was about $20,000 in 1986, and annualized data for 1987 projected about the same amount. Operating data for the previous four years are summarized in Table 9.4 and indicate only one year of marginal profitability.

Table 9.4 Problem Racquetball Club Operating History

	1983	1984	1985	1986
Revenue				
Initiation Fees	$ 60,008	$ 70,503	$101,934	$184,019
Dues	103,160	101,030	141,118	104,982
Guest Fees	862	405	1,850	9,921
Other Income	88,174	76,677	43,831	29,260
Total Gross Revenue	$252,204	$248,615	$288,733	$328,182
Operating Expenses				
Administrative	$ 61,330	$ 66,855	$ 78,696	$ 83,359
Maintenance	14,881	20,065	40,290	27,429
Salary Payroll	33,179	37,806	32,773	53,803
Hourly Payroll	24,732	13,218	19,819	18,287
Marketing	26,551	25,932	28,428	27,844
Supplies	14,443	12,934	15,071	11,622
Utilities	54,481	51,815	59,988	63,400
Property Taxes	23,400	19,931	17,083	20,360
Insurance	4,950	3,943	2,088	2,853
Total Expenses	$257,947	$252,049	$294,236	$308,957
Net Operating Income	$ (5,743)	$ (3,434)	$ (5,503)	$ 19,225
Expense Ratio	102.3%	101.4%	101.9%	94.1%

Analysis

This facility, operating as a racquetball club, did not cover its current debt service obligation, which was about $58,000 annually. The remaining mortgage balance was about $515,000 as of the date of the appraisal.

The appraiser estimated the land value at $250,000; the replacement cost new of the improvements at $1,300,000; and the furniture, fixtures, and equipment at $200,000. These figures resulted in a replacement cost new of $1,750,000.

Given the design, poor historical operating experience, and the adverse market for racquetball clubs in the market area, the appraiser concluded that a substantial deduction for incurable functional obsolescence and external obsolescence was necessary. Under these circumstances, the appraiser gave most weight to the sales comparison approach for valuing this property.

The narrative appraisal report documented extensively the transactions considered and analyzed their relationship to the subject. For illustrative purposes, brief summaries of three sales are presented below.

Sale A. This same age, 12-court, 24,950-square-foot club is located in a similar neighboring community with comparable land values. The sale of this club included a restaurant. Overall, this facility had generated a slight negative net operating income for four years.

Sale price:	$800,000
Per court:	$ 66,667
Per building square foot:	$ 32.06

Sale B. This 8-court, 18,650-square-foot club also was the same age as the subject and had negative net operating income for four years. This sale included similar equipment as the subject, but no snack bar.

Sale price:	$480,000
Per court:	$ 60,000
Per building square foot:	$ 25.74

Sale C. This slightly newer club provided 10 courts within a 16,770-square-foot structure. This facility experienced negative cash flows since its inception and closed three years ago. The bank foreclosed 2 years ago and originally asked $750,000 for the property, including the equipment. It was recently purchased and is being converted to office use. The equipment was sold separately by the bank for $100,000.

Sale price: $360,000
Per building square foot: $21.47

Although all three of these transactions could be considered distressed sales, they were representative of current market conditions. The appraiser discovered that the sale prices of the first two sales and the original asking price for Sale C were all slightly above ($70,000 to $100,000) the remaining mortgage balance on the properties. Sellers were motivated by this consideration while buyers of operating clubs expected to be able to improve profitability. Because of the high conversion costs to other uses (usually offices), relatively low prices were justified for vacant or failing racquetball clubs.

The current value of the subject as an alternative use was between $300,000 and $350,000. These estimates were based on estimated conversion costs and an alternative use income approach. A summary of a simplified income approach for an alternate use as an office building is shown in Table 9.5.

Table 9.5 Income Approach—Alternate Use

26,130 square feet gross × .95 = 24,824 square feet rentable
Estimated Market Rent = $3.50 per square foot per year

Gross Potential Income =		$ 86,884
Vacancy & Collection Loss @ 10%		(8,688)
Effective Gross Income		$ 78,196
Less Expenses:		
Real Estate Taxes	$8,800	
Insurance @ $0.20	$4,965	
Maintenance @ $0.15	$3,724	
Management @ 4%	$3,128	
Total Expenses		$ (20,617)
Net Income		$ 57,579
Capitalized @ 10%		$575,790
Stabilized Value		$576,000
Cost to Cure Renovation @ $10/S.F.		
26,130 square feet × $10/S.F. =		(261,300)
Indicated "As Is" Value		$314,700
Rounded to		$315,000

The indicated value by the income approach for the alternate use of $315,000 is equivalent to $12.06 per square foot of building area. This unit value is considerably below the $21 to $32 per square foot values indicated by the unadjusted comparables sales. Through interviews with buyers, the appraiser discerned that the new operators expected to turn around operations and make a profit from the use of these properties as racquetball clubs. In spite of expectations by these buyers, the appraiser concluded that market evidence did not support such optimistic projections of net income from racquetball club operations.

Nonetheless, the appraiser concluded that the weight of market evidence from the sales comparison approach was compelling. The expectations of buyers in this market tended to support a racquetball club as the highest and best use of the subject. The final recommendation to the current owner was to ask $600,000 ($50,000 per court) for the subject and settled for any amount above the existing loan balance of $515,000.

Case D: Multisport Athletic Club

This multisport athletic club is a prominent facility located in a major metropolitan area of the southeastern United States. Annual population growth in this region is estimated at 2.6%, and the diverse local economy is expanding. Six major competing clubs are located within 11 miles of the subject, and no proposed clubs are located within this market area.

Land Area:	7.85 acres
Building Area:	63,000 square feet
Courts:	14 racquetball/handball courts 2 squash courts 8 outdoor, lighted tennis courts
Other Facilities:	Six-lane, indoor junior Olympics (25 meters) swimming pool; 60-foot diameter outdoor pool; full size gymnasium featuring basketball, volleyball and indoor jogging track; weight training room: separate men's and women's locker rooms including saunas, jacuzzis, massage, steam rooms and tanning beds; nursery, pro shop; and a 94-seat restaurant/lounge.
Age:	9 years
Size of Membership:	Corporate—600 Residential—2,400
Membership Fees:	Initiation—$210 Monthly dues—$95

Operating Results

Net operating income for this club was about $1,600,000 in 1985 and $1,500,000 in 1986. This decline was attributable to higher operating expenses. The appraisal of this facility evaluated a 6,000-square-foot expansion, which would result in a total size of 69,000 feet.

Table 9.6 Multisport Club Operating History

	1986	1985	1984
Operating Revenues:			
Membership Dues	$2,854,533	$2,560,596	$2,086,558
Initiation Fees	?04,301	184,656	212,875
Locker Fees	59,793	53,837	42,326
Other	188,150	180,584	146,535
Total Revenues:	$3,306,777	$2,979,673	$2,488,294
Operating Expenses:			
Payroll and Related Expenses	$ 733,509	$ 598,398	$ 507,436
Administrative and General	268,032	211,520	182,452
Management Fees, Related Party	198,843	81,000	139,800
Marketing	194,549	119,061	79,478
Energy Costs	169,597	168,689	177,557
Property Operations and Maintenance	118,516	94,534	76,765
Insurance and Property Taxes	157,105	117,289	71,984
Total Expenses	$1,840,251	$1,391,491	$1,235,472
Net Income	$1,466,526	$1,588,182	$1,252,822
Operating Expense Ratio	55.7%	46.7%	49.7%

Analysis

No competitive clubs were located within 3.5 miles of the subject, where over 50% of all members resided. The existing market penetration within this radius was about 1% of total population. The average household income in this area was $35,500; and 66% of the labor force are engaged in executive, managerial, professional, or administrative occupations. Over 1,000,000 square feet of office space is also located nearby.

The appraisers projected a stabilized membership of 3,200 in 1990. Using a 12.5% reversion capitalization rate and a 14.5% discount rate, the appraisers concluded a discounted value of the real estate, personal assets, and the business of $14,900,000 and a stabilized value of $16,000,000.

Table 9.7 Multisport Club Discounted Cash Flow Projections

	1987 3,000 Memberships $1,140 Annual Dues			1988 3,000 Memberships $1,186 Annual Dues			1989 3,100 Memberships $1,233 Annual Dues			1990 3,200 Memberships $1,282 Annual Dues		
	Amount	Ratio	Amount/Mem.	Amount	Ratio	Amount/Mem.	Amount	Ratio	Amount/Mem.	Amount	Ratio	Amount/Mem.
Revenues:												
Membership Dues	$3,420,000	87.4%	$1,140	$3,557,000	87.4%	$1,186	$3,822,000	87.2%	$1,233	$4,104,000	87.2%	$1,283
Initiation Fees	226,000	5.8%	75	235,000	5.8%	79	254,000	5.8%	83	277,000	5.9%	88
Guest Fees	83,000	2.1%	28	86,000	2.1%	30	97,000	2.2%	30	101,000	2.1%	31
Locker Fees	66,000	1.7%	22	69,000	1.7%	23	74,000	1.7%	24	79,000	1.7%	25
Other Operating Income	120,000	3.1%	40	125,000	3.1%	42	135,408	3.1%	44	145,367	3.1%	45
Total—Revenues	$3,915,000	100.0%	$1,305	$4,072,000	100.0%	$1,357	$4,382,408	100.0%	$1,414	$4,706,367	100.0%	$1,471
Operating Expenses:												
Management Fees	235,000	6.0%	$78	244,000	6.0%	$81	263,000	6.0%	$85	282,000	6.0%	$88
Payroll & Related	783,000	20.0%	261	814,000	20.0%	271	920,000	21.0%	297	988,000	21.0%	309
Admin. & General	313,000	8.0%	104	326,000	8.0%	109	351,000	8.0%	113	377,000	8.0%	118
Marketing	235,000	6.0%	78	244,000	6.0%	81	219,000	5.0%	71	235,000	5.0%	73
Utilities	196,000	5.0%	65	204,000	5.0%	68	219,000	5.0%	71	282,000	6.0%	88
Repairs & Maintenance	157,000	4.0%	52	163,000	4.0%	54	197,000	4.5%	64	212,000	4.5%	66
Total—Operating Expenses	$1,919,000	49.0%	$640	$1,995,000	49.0%	$665	$2,169,000	49.5%	$700	$2,376,000	50.5%	$743
Income Before Fixed Charges	$1,996,000	51.0%	$665	$2,077,000	51.0%	$692	$2,213,408	50.5%	$714	$2,330,367	49.5%	$718
Fixed Charges:												
Real Estate & Property Taxes	$98,000	2.5%	$33	$101,920	2.5%	$34	$105,997	2.4%	$34	$110,237	2.3%	$34
Building & Contents Insurance	78,000	2.0%	26	81,040	2.0%	27	84,365	1.9%	27	87,739	1.9%	27
Total	$176,000	4.5%	$59	$183,040	4.5%	$61	$190,362	4.3%	$61	$197,976	4.2%	$62
Income Before Reserve	$1,820,000	46.5%	$607	$1,893,960	46.5%	$631	$2,023,046	46.2%	$653	$2,132,391	45.3%	$666
Reserves for Replacement: Furniture, Fixtures & Equip.	$39,000	1.0%	$13	$61,000	1.5%	$20	$88,000	2.0%	$28	$94,000	2.0%	$29
Net Cash Flow	$1,781,000	45.1%	$594	$1,832,960	45.0%	$611	$1,935,046	44.2%	$624	$2,038,391	43.3%	$637
P.V. Factor @ 14.5%	.87336			.77276			.66617					
P.V. Cash Flow	$1,555,459			$1,398,112			$1,289,065					

165

Table 9.8 Multisport Club Discounted Present Value Calculations

Gross Reversionary Price ($2,038,391 @ 12.5% Cap Rate)	$16,307,128
Less Cost of Sales @ 2%	(326,143)
Net Reversionary Proceeds	$15,980,985
Year 3 P.V. Factor @ 14.5% Discounted Rate	× 0.66617
Present Value of Reversion	$10,646,053
Present Value of Cash Flow @ 14.5% Discounted Rate (See Figure 9.6)	$ 4,242,636
Total Net Present Value	$14,888,689
Rounded to	$14,900,000

Case E: Tennis/Mixed-Use Project

Tennis clubs and health clubs often are found as part of mixed-use developments. In many cases, these recreational facilities are part of a residential or time-share development. Case E is primarily a tennis club with 20 luxury hotel units. It is located in an affluent suburban community in the southwestern United States where a large portion of the work force is employed in management and technical occupations. Membership in this club has declined slightly over the past 5 years as competition has increased. The purpose of the appraisal was to evaluate a 1,480-square-foot addition that will increase the areas devoted to weight training and aerobics. These improvements are expected to make the subject club more competitive in the market.

Land Area:	11.0 acres
Courts:	21 lighted tennis courts, including 13 lighted outdoor courts, 4 indoor courts and a championship tournament court; 6 air-conditioned handball/racquetball courts
Buildings:	Clubhouse, 252-seat restaurant/bar, 20-unit luxury hotel
Other Facilities	Junior-olympic heated outdoor swimming pool; separate men's and women's locker rooms including jacuzzis, steam rooms and saunas; pro shop; nursery; weight rooms; aerobics rooms; lobby; offices; and conference room.
Age:	12 years

Size of Membership:

774 — full privilege
133 — racquetball
227 — social/fitness
1,134 — Total

Membership Fees:

	Initiation	Monthly
Full Privilege—	$1,250	$112
Racquetball—	$ 600	$ 75
Social/Fitness—	$ 300	$ 62

Projected Operating Results

The appraisers were provided with good historical operating data for the subject. These figures are summarized in Table 9.8. In addition to the health club components, the appraiser had to consider net operating results from the hotel, restaurant lease, and pro shop. Although revenues were relatively easy to calculate, separate accounting of expenses for these profit centers was not available. In this case, the appraiser found the application of overall operating expense ratios to be historically consistent and reasonable for valuation purposes.

Operating results indicated that the room rates for the hotel ranged from $72.00 to $77.00, and the average occupancy rate for 1985 was 81.9%. For the first 13 weeks of 1986, the occupancy rate was 72.1%, but this period historically was below the annual average in the subject. The restaurant and cocktail lounge was leased for 25 years commencing in 1977. The lease requires a guaranteed rent of $7,000 per month or 6% of gross annual sales, whichever is greater. The restaurant also pays utilities and a percentage of taxes in the future. At the time of the appraisal, the pro shop was rented out at $850 per month plus a percentage of property taxes and a handling fee. The lease was to terminate within the first year of the appraisal, and the management indicated it would not be renewed. Subsequent to the renovation of this facility, one centralized desk would handle hotel registrations, tennis check-ins, and sales of pro shop merchandise.

Gross Revenues

For valuation purposes, revenues were divided into dues income, membership services, food and beverage, merchandise sales, guest room rentals, restaurant rent, and miscellaneous.

During 1985 total gross revenues amounted to $2,326,000. The appraiser's analysis of projected dues under an expanded club concept are shown in Table 9.9.

Table 9.9 Tennis/Mixed-Use Project: Summary of Revenue and Expenses ($000)

Revenue:	1983*	%	1984	%	1985	%	1986**	%
Dues	$ 749	51.8	$1,136	51.5	$1,237	53.2	$304	58.0
Services	162	11.2	263	11.9	292	12.6	69	13.2
Food & Beverage	159	11.0	235	10.8	22	0.9	5	0.9
Merchandise	58	4.0	85	3.8	—	—	—	—
Rent	235	16.3	357	16.2	403	17.3	80	15.3
Miscellaneous	83	5.7	129	5.8	372	16.0	66	12.6
	$1,446	100.0	$2,205	100.0	$2,326	100.0	$524	100.0
Expenses:								
Food & Beverage	$ 5	0.3	$ 8	0.4	$ 9	0.4	$ 1	0.2
Salaries & Wages	346	23.9	499	22.6	575	24.7	122	23.3
Commissions	244	16.9	371	16.8	390	16.8	77	14.7
Contract Services	34	2.4	48	2.2	48	2.1	10	1.9
Rent, Repair, & Maintenance	21	1.4	32	1.5	35	1.5	6	1.1
Printing, Art, & Decorating	15	1.0	17	0.8	25	1.1	7	1.3
Postage & Freight	5	0.3	7	0.3	8	0.3	—	—
Supplies & Tools	24	1.7	48	2.2	60	2.6	11	2.1
Credit & Collections	12	0.8	7	0.3	6	0.2	—	—
Utilities	85	5.9	142	6.4	149	6.4	41	7.8
Telephone	21	1.5	34	1.5	35	1.5	7	1.3
Legal & Professional	4	0.3	11	0.5	10	0.4	1	0.2
Consulting Fee	37	2.6	54	2.4	54	2.3	12	2.3
Taxes, Licenses, & Permits	49	3.4	83	3.8	129	5.5	31	5.9
Insurance	7	0.5	10	0.5	18	0.8	6	1.2
Uniforms, Laundry	11	0.8	20	0.9	27	1.2	5	1.0
Miscellaneous	31	2.1	55	2.5	65	2.8	11	2.1
Total	$ 951	65.8	$1,446	65.6	$1,643	70.6	$348	66.4
Net Income:	$ 495	34.2	$ 759	34.4	$ 683	29.4	$176	33.6

* = 37 Weeks

** = 13 Weeks

Currently the club has 775 full privilege members, 133 racquetball members, and 227 social/fitness members. The appraiser projected that the expansion of the club would allow the sale of the remaining memberships allotment to reach a total membership of 1,375. The projected full membership comprised 775 full privilege members, 150 racquetball club members, and 450 social/fitness members.

With an allowance for a 3% collection loss and contingency allowance, total revenues in this category in one year will amount to $1,466,058, as follows:

```
775 full privilege  @ $112/Mo. × 12 = $1,041,600
150 racquetball     @ $ 75/Mo. × 12 = $  135,000
450 social/fitness  @ $ 62/Mo. × 12 = $  334,800
Subtotal                              $1,511,400
3% vacancy/contingency allowance      $   45,342
Total revenue                         $1,466,058
```

Membership Services. This category is expressed as a percentage of dues income. It amounted to 22.7% in the first 13 weeks of 1986, 23.6% in 1985, 23.1% in 1984, and 21.6% for 37 weeks in 1983. The average for all these categories is 22.75% of dues income, equivalent to $333,528 for valuation purposes (22.75% × $1,466,058 = $333,538).

Food and Beverage. This is a very minor category; it amounted to $22,000 in 1985 and $5,000 for the first 13 weeks of 1986. The projection for valuation purposes was $25,000.

Merchandise Sales. On termination of the existing pro shop lease, the management was expected to control and operate this department. For valuation purposes, the best evidence for a future estimate was its performance in 1983 and 1984. During those years, merchandise sales amounted to 7.7% of dues revenue for 37 weeks in 1983 and 7.5% for 1984. The appraiser projected a rate of 7.6% of projected dues revenue or a sales volume of $111,420 (7.6% × $1,466,058 = $111,420).

Guest Room Rentals. This category amounted to $357,000 in 1984 and $403,000 in 1985. The appraiser projected an average room rate of $75.00 and average occupancy rate of 77% to arrive at a stabilized figure for valuation purposes of $421,575 ($75.00 per day × 365 days × 20 rooms × 77% = $421,575).

Restaurant Rent. This category represents a combination of guaranteed rent, percentage rent, and other payments for operating expenses. The current budget for the first 13 weeks of 1986 provides for a flat rental of $19,386 and percentage rent of $3,500; the actual performance was slightly below this estimate, but with a larger number of members in the future it was expected to be a conservative figure for valuation purposes. On a full-year basis, the above budget figure for one fourth of a year is equivalent to approximately $91,500 in revenue per year from this category.

Miscellaneous Income. This category varied substantially over the past three years as a percentage of dues revenue because of a continued redefining of its elements. During 1983 (37 weeks), miscellaneous income was 7.1% of dues income; it amounted to 11.4% in 1984, 30.1% in 1985, and 21.7% in 1986. For valuation purposes, the appraiser considered 11% of dues income a conservative estimate of total revenue from this category. This amounted to $161,266 (11% of $1,466,058 = $161,266).

Total Revenue Estimates. Total revenue estimates for valuation purposes was $2,610,000, as shown below:

Dues revenue	$1,466,058
Membership services	$ 333,528
Food and beverage	$ 25,000
Merchandise sales	$ 111,420
Guest room rentals	$ 421,575
Restaurant revenue	$ 91,500
Miscellaneous	$ 161,266
Total	$2,610,347
Called	$2,610,000

Operating Expenses

The appraiser felt it was unnecessary to analyze in detail each one of the expense categories. Rather, he felt it would be more accurate to study the historical expense ratios. Total operating expenses as a percentage of total revenues, as summarized in Table 9.8, amounted to 65.8% for 37 weeks in 1983, 65.6% in 1984, 70.6% in 1985, and 66.4% for the first 13 weeks of 1986. This expense ratio range is highly consistent and shows great stability of management. The mean for the above periods is 67.1%. For valuation purposes it provided an allowance of $1,751,310 for operating expenses (67.1% × $2,610,000 = $1,751,310).

Net Income

The difference between gross revenue of $2,610,000 and expenses of $1,751,310 amounts to net income for valuation purposes of $858,690.

Capitalization Rate

Because of the unusual combination of characteristics for Case E, the capitalization rate was derived from a combination of sources with primary weight given to the 1983 purchase price divided by the 1984 net income. The acquisition of the subject property based upon a net income of $759,000 in 1984 resulted in a capitalization rate of 10.4%. Other comparisons would include typical capitalization rates of 10% to 12% for hotels and motels and 12% to 14% for most racquetball sports/spa facilities. The appraiser concluded that an appropriate rate for the subject should be 11%.

Total Indicated Value

Based upon application of an overall rate of 11% to the projected net income of $858,690, the indicated valuation was $7,800,000 ($858,690 divided by 11% = $7,806,272, called $7,800,000).

Conclusion

The appraiser concluded a value by the cost approach of $7,680,000. Only one sale of a large multisport club facility was discovered. This club did not have a full-service restaurant nor a hotel. This sale reported a gross revenue multiplier (GRM) of 2.83. Adjusting this figure upward to 3.0 because of the clear superiority of the subject, the resulting value indication was $7,830,000 (GRM of 3.0 × $2,610,000 = $7,830,000). The appraiser did not feel that either of these indicators of value had enough substantiation to stand on their own. Nonetheless, they did provide support for the value indication by the income approach.

Most competitive facilities in the vicinity of the subject did not have tennis courts. This feature helped to make the subject unique. In addition, the subject has 20 hotel rooms and a full food and beverage restaurant. Because of these conditions, it was extremely difficult to compare "typical" racquet sport or fitness facilities to derive units of comparison relative to rate structure, number of memberships, operating costs, and so forth. Thus, the appraiser relied upon historical operating results from the subject and applied appropriate appraisal techniques.

Case F: Traditional Health Spa

Many spas appeal to a nationwide market; and their locations, although weighted toward the South and West, do not greatly influence valuation. In cases known to the authors, income projections are based almost exclusively on historical operating performance. Depending upon the facility, it usually is difficult to separate the lodging component from the spa portion of the property. Income is generated from overnight (usually weekly) guest fees, which include lodging, food and beverages, use of the facilities, and various personal services. The following example of a luxury operation is provided for illustrative purposes.

Land Area:	4.9 acres
Building Area:	56,000 square feet
Guest Rooms:	36
Other Facilities:	Outdoor swimming pool, exercise rooms, massage/treatment rooms, dining room, various lounges, tennis courts
Age:	18 years
Fees:	$2,200 per week per guest

Operating Results

Occupancy rates at this spa averaged 96.8% during the 5 years prior to its appraisal in 1986. During that time, gross revenues increased from about $1,600,000 to $3,100,000, an increase of over 90%, or about 12% per year compounded. Operating expenses also increased but more rapidly than income. The expense ratio increased from 61% in 1982 to 73% in 1986 and appeared stabilized at that time. During that period, management provided more services and increased the ratio of staff per guest to about 3.5. This extremely high ratio enabled the spa to provide outstanding personal service which aided its reputation. The strategy helped the subject spa to maintain its position in the market while net operating income increased 20% in five years.

The appraiser valued this spa using a 4-year cash flow projection. Income was projected to increase at historical rates while the most recent expense ratio remained constant. Given the high occupancy and established market for this nationally known facility, the appraiser employed an 11.5% reversion capitalization rate and a 14% discount rate. The concluded value of the income approach was $10,300,000, whereas the value by the cost approach was $8,500,000. This difference of $1,800,000 was attributed to the goodwill or business value of the spa.

Table 9.10 Health Spa: Summary of Income and Expenses

	Dollars ($000 Omitted)					Percentages					Pro Forma
	1982	1983	1984	1985	1986	1982	1983	1984	1985	1986	
Income:											
Sales:											
Merchandise	229	272	323	374	446	8.7	9.5	10.3	10.6	11.8	
Cost of Goods Sold	132	154	195	201	245	5.0	5.4	6.2	5.7	6.5	
Gross Income	97	118	128	173	201	3.7	4.1	4.1	4.9	5.3	5.0
Fees:											
Enrollment	2,510	2,706	2,992	3,292	3,527	95.1	95.0	94.9	94.0	93.6	
Health Care	5	4	5	5	5	0.2	0.2	0.2	0.1	0.1	
Beauty Care	12	8	10	11	12	0.4	0.3	0.3	0.3	0.3	
Miscellaneous	15	12	16	23	23	0.6	0.4	0.5	0.7	0.7	
Gross Income	2,542	2,730	3,023	3,331	3,567	96.3	95.9	95.9	95.1	94.7	95.0
Total Income	2,639	2,848	3,151	3,504	3,768	100.0	100.0	100.0	100.0	100.0	100.0
Expenses:											
Salaries & Wages	874	965	1,139	1,287	1,387	33.1	33.9	36.1	36.7	36.8	36.5
Payroll Burden	101	104	163	194	255	3.8	3.7	5.2	5.5	6.8	6.0
Taxes	29	27	34	32	31	1.1	0.9	1.1	0.9	0.8	0.9
Advertising	28	38	17	28	88	1.1	1.3	0.5	0.8	2.3	1.0
Travel & Promotion	12	9	12	13	10	0.4	0.3	0.4	0.4	0.3	0.4
Rents	12	20	14	16	26	0.4	0.7	0.4	0.5	0.7	0.6
Professional Fees	94	118	113	119	146	3.6	4.1	3.6	3.4	3.9	3.7
Repairs & Maintenance	76	107	113	166	129	2.9	3.8	3.6	4.7	3.4	3.4
Operating Supplies	245	252	289	361	371	9.3	8.9	9.2	10.3	9.8	10.0
Utilities	115	123	146	175	203	4.4	4.3	4.6	5.0	5.4	5.5
Insurance	25	51	83	50	50	0.9	1.8	2.6	1.4	1.3	1.0
Other	—	86	50	20	56	—	3.0	1.6	0.6	1.5	1.0
Total Expenses	1,611	1,900	2,173	2,461	2,752	61.0	66.7	68.9	70.2	73.0	70.0
Net Income Before Capital Charges	1,028	948	978	1,043	1,016	39.0	33.3	31.0	29.8	27.0	30.0

Table 9.11 Summary of Health Spa Discounted Cash Flow Analysis

	1987	1988	1989	1990
Total Gross Income (7%/yr)	$ 4,032	$ 4,314	$ 4,616	$ 4,939
Expenses (70%)	2,822	3,020	3,231	3,457
Net Income	1,210	1,294	1,385	1,482
Reserves for Replacements @ 3%	121	129	138	148
Net Cash Flow	1,089	1,165	1,247	1,334
P.V. Factor @ 14%	0.8772	0.7695	0.6750	
P.V. Cash Flow	955	896	842	
Gross Reversionary Price (Based on 11.5% Cap Rate)				$11,600
Cost of Sales @ 2.5%				290
Net Reversionary Proceeds				$11,310
Total P.V. Cash Flow	$ 2,693			
P.V. Reversion	7,634			
Total Present Value	$10,327,000			

Conclusion

10

The two most prominent characteristics of the health and fitness club industry are diversity and change. Very few hard and fast rules apply to these types of facilities and businesses. This book has described a wide variety of clubs, in terms of both their physical characteristics and services. Many different combinations are evident in the marketplace, as illustrated by the examples in Chapter 9.

The diversity of clubs has occurred through an evolutionary process. Entrepreneurs have experimented with different types of facilities and services in response to perceived shifts of demand. The result has been a myriad of choices for consumers. A secondary consequence for appraisers, developers, and lenders has been a convoluted market that is difficult to analyze.

This book has focused on the diversity and change in the industry. In fact, the primary purpose for this book is that the original published in 1978 was out of date. The information this book contains is expected to benefit the appraisal, development, and lending communities when they venture into analyzing recreational facilities. At best, however, this book can serve only as a general guide based on the analytical principles it outlines. Market conditions, facility types, and data resources will continue to change.

Observations of the market have led the authors to speculate about future trends in the health club industry. Future industry changes will be derived, as they have in the past, from market conditions. One of the most important factors influencing the market is demographics.

Many industries in the United States are influenced by the so-called "baby boomers," or those born between 1946 and 1964. These Americans are now entering their prime earning years and should have disposable income that enables them to join clubs. Survey data demonstrate, however, that the prime target market for most clubs is the 21 to 40 age bracket. As the proportion of the population aged 40+ grows, different marketing strategies will be necessary to maintain profitability.

One of the resulting trends will be the increasing family orientation of clubs. Most new single-purpose clubs are being constructed with daycare facilities. In addition, clubs are adding special programs for youths. These include after school swimming classes, targeted weight training sessions for teenagers, and the addition of exercise equipment designed for children. This trend may be particularly strong in sunbelt states. Between 1980 and 2000, 5 states—California, Texas, Florida, North Carolina and Arizona—will account for 73% of the national gain in children under age 14.[1]

Capture of middle-aged adults has been difficult for most health clubs to achieve. In addition to developing a family orientation, clubs are adding programs to attract this segment of the market. One of the most prominent marketing activities targets corporate membership. These activities are expected to continue and expand. Another market segment that appeals to many adults is the "deconditioned market". Clubs may add more low-stress workout programs, such as aqua aerobics. Conflicts between older members and young, attractive, and fit members probably will remain unless separate facilities are developed. This market segment probably is not large enough in most market areas to justify such an expense, but specially designed programs for senior citizens may prove profitable for some clubs.

In addition to demographic pressures, the authors foresee changes in industry structures. In response to demographic and demand shifts, the multisport athletic facility probably will become more dominant in the market. These types of clubs appeal to a variety of market segments because of the wide array of facilities and programs they offer. Multisport clubs are likely to be in the best position to respond to changing conditions.

Even considering successful responses to changing market conditions, market analysts will remain wary of this industry. More club failures will continue to receive publicity in most metropolitan areas. Recreational club membership is paid from discretionary income in most households. During times of economic difficulty or a recession, club membership probably would be one of the first items a family or individual would eliminate. Clubs located in areas dominated by a single industry may be particularly vulnerable.

The most important facet that will determine profitability of well-located and appropriately targeted clubs is management. Day-to-day operations are most important to membership retention and also contribute strongly to sales. This aspect of the club is particularly difficult to judge for outsiders, such as appraisers or lenders. Chapter 5 of this book describes some of the critical factors that are necessary for good management.

An industry trend that may become more prominent in the future is health club chains. Most clubs are privately held but a few chains comprise a significant market share. The most well-known is the Health and Tennis Corporation of America, which is a subsidiary of Bally, Inc. Other publicly traded clubs include U.S. Health, Inc., Living Well, Inc., and T.H.E. Fitness Centers, Inc. Chain clubs should be better able to absorb cyclical downturns of individual clubs because they have a broader base and tend to be better capitalized than individually owned clubs. The chain club also should be able to provide superior management assistance to club operators. Chains should provide training for managers and sharing of information and advertising materials. These positive influences will be balanced, however, by the negatives associated with larger organizations, such as bureaucratic inefficiencies. Nonetheless, the authors foresee chains occupying a more prominent market position in the future.

End Notes

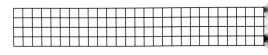

Chapter 1

[1] Steve Huntley and Ronald A. Taylor, "Keeping in Shape—Everybody's Doing It," *U.S. News & World Report* (August 13, 1984), pp. 24-25.

[2] "Staying Fit—On The Job," *PSA Magazine* (July 1987), pp. 26-27.

[3] Adam Paul Wisman, "The Business Of Staying Fit Keeps In Step," *U.S. News & World Report* (August 11, 1986), p. 56.

[4] Alvin P. Sanoff, "Business Gets Healthy From Athletics, Too," *U.S. News & World Report* (August 13, 1984), pp. 26-27.

[5] Bob Gatty, "How Business Works Out," *Nation's Business* (July 1985), pp. 18-24.

[6] Sanoff, pp. 26-27.

Chapter 2

[1] Roger Cox, "50 Greatest U.S. Tennis Resorts," *Tennis* (November 1984), pp. 52-57.

[2] Suzanne Hildreth, "Getting More Bounce Out of Basketball," *IRSA Club Business* (July 1987), pp. 46-49.

[3] "On Sports—Wallyball," *The Wall Street Journal*, February 14, 1986, p. 19.

[4] Suzanne Hildreth, "The Swimming Success," *IRSA Club Business* (May 1987) pp. 78-80.

[5] International Racquet Sports Association, *Profiles of Success—1987 State of the Industry Report* (Brookline: IRSA, 1987), p. 13.

[6] Kelly Donahoe, "Planning Your Pool Without Going Off the Deep End," *IRSA Club Business* (July 1987), pp. 41-45.

[7] John Dietrich and Susan Waggoner, *The Complete Health Club Handbook* (New York: Crown Publishers Inc., 1983), p. 162.

[8] Anastasia Toutexis, "Watch the Bouncing Body," *Time* (June 30, 1986), p. 74.

[9] Dietrich and Waggoner, p. 149.

[10] "Fitness Centers: Profit Centers?" *Hospitals* (July 20, 1986), pp. 52-53.

[11] Daniel Cooke, "The Business of Balance: Wellness Moves Towards the Spa Experience," *IRSA Club Business* (June 1987), pp. 57-65.

[12] Diane Tegmeyer, "Getting Physical at the Airport," *Working Women* (July 1985), pp. 51-52.

[13] Sharon Nelton, "The Over-50 Exerciser Finds a Couple of Allies," *Nation's Business* (June 1985), p. 54.

[14] Virginia Inman, "Upstarts," *Inc.* (February 1986), p. 22.

[15] Babes in Exerciseland," *Life* (February 1987), p. 30.

Chapter 3

[1] Linda K. Monroe, "Fitness Centers as Amenities," *Buildings* (July 1986), pp. 60-63.

[2] *Ibid.*, p. 62.

[3] Dietrich and Waggoner, pp. 231-232.

[4] *Ibid.*, pp. 238-240.

[5] *Ibid.*, p. 149.

Chapter 4

[1] Game Plan, Inc., *Why People Play—A Report on the Sport of Tennis* (New York: United States Tennis Association, Inc., 1987), p. 19.

[2] *Ibid.*, p. 80.

[3] *Ibid.*, p. 59.

[4] Game Plan, Inc., *Why People Join—A Market Research Study for Racquet and Fitness Clubs* (Brookline: IRSA, 1985), pp. 16-20.

[5] Dietrich and Waggoner, pp. 101-103.

[6] Game Plan, Inc., *Why People Join*, pp. 16-20.

[7] *Ibid.*

[8] Gallup Opinion Polls, *Gallup Leisure Activities Index 1986* (Princeton: 1986), p. 90.

[9] Game Plan, Inc., *Why People Join*, p. 61.

[10] *Ibid.*, p. 64.

[11] *Ibid.*, p. 65.

[12] Charley Swayne, "Know Your Trade Area," *IRSA Guide to Sales & Marketing* (1986), p. 41.

[13] *Ibid.*

[14] *Ibid.*

[15] *Ibid.*

[16] *Ibid.*

Chapter 5

[1] IRSA, *Profiles of Success*, p. 6.

[2] *Ibid.*

[3] Catherine Masterson, "Business As Usual: A Perilous Road?" *IRSA Club Business* (June 1987), pp. 38-39.

[4] "Ten Steps to Targeting Your Market," *IRSA Guide to Sales & Marketing* (Brookline: IRSA, 1986), pp. 7-8.

[5] *Ibid.*

[6] "How to Maximize Your Sales Staff," *IRSA Guide to Sales & Marketing* (Brookline: IRSA, 1986), pp. 81-83.

[7] Dietrich and Waggoner, p. 257.

[8] *Ibid.*, pp. 258-260.

[9] Masterson, p. 37.

[10] Dietrich and Waggoner, pp. 51-53.

[11] *Ibid.*

[12] "How to Calculate the Amount of Liability Insurance You Need," *Club Industry* (April 1988), pp. 52-53.

[13] "FTC Staff Takes It Easy on Health-Spa Operations," *Consumer Reports* (November 1985), p. 643.

[14] Richard B. Schmitt, "Fiscal Fitness: Efforts to Regulate Health Clubs Fail to End Abuses," *Wall Street Journal*, April 3, 1987, p. 33.

[15] *Ibid.*

[16] *Ibid.*

[17] *Ibid.*

[18] Suzanne Hildreth, "Why the Storefront Myth Won't Work," *IRSA Club Business* (July 1987), pp. 35-39.

[19] *Ibid.*

[20] "FTC Terminates Health Spa Rulemaking Procedure; Directs Staff to Explore Additional Law Enforcement Options," *FTC News* (Washington, D.C.: Federal Trade Commission, December 19, 1985).

[21] Schmitt, p. 33.

[22] Bob Rawson, "Looking Into Locker Rooms," *IRSA Club Business* (July 1987), p. 69.

Chapter 6

[1] Michelle Roch, "One, Two, Three Invest," *Canadian Banker* (April 1987), pp. 6-12.

Chapter 7

[1] Ron Lawrence, *Club Location—A Site Analysis Study* (Brookline: IRSA, 1984), p. 6.

[2] Game Plan, Inc., *Why People Join*, p. 10.

[3] *Ibid.*, pp. 11-12.

[4] U.S. Bureau of the Census, *Statistical Abstract of the United States: 1987*, 107th edition (Washington, D.C., 1986) p. 431.

[5] Ron Lawrence, "Club Location—Setting Your Sites on the Right Site," *IRSA Club Business* (April 1984), pp. 24-26.

Chapter 10

[1] M. Leanne Lachman and Dan Martin, "Changing Demographics Shape Tomorrow's Real Estate Markets," *Urban Land* (November 1987), pp. 8-11.

Select Bibliography

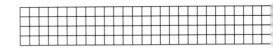

Books

Annual Statement Studies. Philadelphia: Robert Morris Associates, 1986.

The Appraisal of Real Estate, ninth edition. Chicago: American Institute of Real Estate Appraisers, 1987.

Babcock, Judy, and Kennedy, Judy. *The Spa Book.* New York: Crown Publishers, Inc., 1983.

Caro, Richard M. Jr. *Financial Management.* Brookline: International Racquet Sports Association, 1986.

Clubs in Town and Country. Houston: Pannell Kerr Forster, 1986.

Dietrich, John, and Waggoner, Susan. *The Complete Health Club Handbook.* New York: Simon & Schuster, 1983.

Gallup Opinion Poll. *Gallup Leisure Activities Index 1986.* Princeton, 1986.

Game Plan, Inc. *Why People Join: A Market Research Study for Racquet and Fitness Clubs*, Brookline: International Racquet Sports Association, 1985.

Game Plan, Inc. *Why People Play: A Report on the Sport of Tennis.* Lexington: United States Tennis Association, 1987.

Gimmy, Arthur E. *Tennis Clubs and Racquet Sport Projects: A Guide to Appraisal, Market Analysis, Development and Financing.* Chicago: American Institute of Real Estate Appraisers, 1978.

Gimmy, Arthur E., and Boehm, Michael. *Elderly Housing: A Guide to Appraisal, Market Analysis, Development and Financing.* Chicago: American Institute of Real Estate Appraisers, 1988.

IRSA Guide to Sales & Marketing. Brookline: International Racquet Sports Association, 1986.

Judd, Patricia, and Richards, Timothy. *Uniform Reporting System for Racquet and Fitness Clubs.* Brookline: International Racquet Sports Association, 1985.

Lawrence, Ron. *Club Location: A Site Analysis Study.* Brookline: International Racquet Sports Association, 1984.

Marshall & Swift. *Marshall Valuation Service.* Los Angeles: Marshall and Swift Publication Company, 1987.

1982-1983 Nationwide Recreation Survey. Washington, D.C.: U.S. Department of the Interior, National Park Service, 1986.

Profiles of Success: 1987 State of the Industry Report. Brookline: International Racquet Sports Association, 1987.

Recreational Development Handbook. Washington, D.C.: Urban Land Institute, 1981.

Report and Recommendations to the President of the United States. Washington, D.C.: President's Commission on Americans Outdoors, 1986.

Rushmore, Stephen. *Hotels, Motels, and Restaurants—Valuations and Market Studies.* Chicago: American Institute of Real Estate Appraisers, 1983.

Statistical Abstract of the United States: 1987. 107th edition. Washington, D.C.: U.S. Bureau of the Census, 1986.

Vodak, Paul. *Exercise—The Why and the How.* Palo Alto: Bull Publishing Company, 1980.

Articles in Journals, Periodicals, and Newspapers

A.C. Nielsen Company. *News Release.* Northbrook, IL, 1982.

———. "Sports Participation 1982." 1982.

American Amateur Racquetball Association. "Media/Market Bulletin." 1987.

Baron, Ron. "Legal Protection: Guarding Against Lawsuits." *IRSA Club Business,* May 1987, pp. 88-89.

Baun, Bill, and Williams, Kathy. "Tenneco: Building on Corporate Quality Through Good Health." *Management Review*, June 1985, pp. 51-54.

Breen, Terry. "Marketing Is Key to a Successful Fitness Facility." *Hotel & Motel Management*, March 30, 1987, pp. 22-23.

Bryant, Barbara. "Built for Excitement." *American Demographics*, March 1987, pp. 38-42.

Caro, Richard M., Jr. "Winning the Real Estate Tax Battle and the War." *IRSA Club Business*, June 1987, pp. 47-49. (Part II, July 1987, pp. 55-57).

Cato, Dr. Bertha. "Promoting Fitness." *Parks and Recreation*, July 1984, pp. 53-61.

Chaffin, James, Jr. "The Snowmass Club." *Urban Land*, March 1985, pp. 20-23.

Cinque, Chris. "Aerobic Instructor Certification: Standards at Last." *Physician & Sportsmedicine*, December 1986, pp. 171-174.

Clayton, Ken. "Hotels Fight for Fitness Market." *Marketing*, December 4, 1986, pp. 46-48.

Cooke, Daniel. "The Business of Balance: Wellness Moves Towards the Spa Experience." *IRSA Club Business*, June 1987, pp. 57-65.

———. "Packaging for Prestige: The Tennis Advantage." *IRSA Club Business*, July 1987, pp. 62-67.

———. "Vision Beyond the Box." *IRSA Club Business*, May 1987, pp. 73-77.

Copeland, J., Springen, K., and Donovan, JR. "Are Health Clubs Risky?" *Newsweek*, February 17, 1986, p. 62.

Cox, Roger. "50 Greatest U.S. Tennis Resorts." *Tennis*, November 1984, pp. 52-58.

———. "Get Ready for Designer Resorts." *Tennis*, February 1987, pp. 123-125.

Donahue, Kelly. "Planning Your Pool Without Going Off the Deep End." *IRSA Club Business*, July 1987, pp. 41-45.

Eberhart, Cheryl. "Keeping Fit: Expanding Fitness Areas Are in High Demand." *Hotel & Motel Management*, February 3, 1986, pp. 18-20.

Elmer-DeWitt, Philip. "Extra Years for Extra Effort." *Time*, March 17, 1986, p. 66.

Federal Trade Commission. *FTC News Releases*. Washington, D.C., 1985.

Fitness Industry. "1986 Market Report." 1986.

Flanagan, Barbara. "Warm Up, Cool Down." *Progressive Architecture*, September 1984, pp. 128-132.

Garrett, Spencer. "There Are Two Sides to Every Story." *IRSA Club Business*, May 1987, pp. 86-87.

Gatty, Bob. "How Fitness Works Out: Helping Employees Keep Fit Improves Health and Job Performance." *Nation's Business*, July 1985, pp. 18-24.

Hildreth, Suzanne. "The ACSM Seal of Approval: Who's Fit to Teach Fitness." *IRSA Club Business*, June 1987, pp. 72-75.

————. "Regional Associations: Plugging In to a Network of Ideas." *IRSA Club Business*, May 1987, pp. 40-47.

————. "The Swimming Success." *IRSA Club Business*, May 1987, pp. 78-80.

————. "Why the Storefront Myth Won't Work." *IRSA Club Business*, July 1987, pp. 35-39.

Hollandsworth, Skip. "Working Out While Stopping Over." *Women's Sports and Fitness*, November 1985, p. 47.

Huntley, Steve. "Keeping In Shape—Everybody's Doing It." *U.S. News & World Report*, August 13, 1984, pp. 24-25.

Inman, Virginia. "Upstarts." *Inc.*, February 1986, p. 22.

Jensen, Joyce. "Half of Consumers in Fitness Programs." *Modern Healthcare*, February 28, 1986, p. 42.

Kilburg, Patricia, and Strischek, Dev. "Lending to Health Clubs." *Journal of Commercial Bank Lending* (Robert Morris Associates), August 1985, pp. 8-21.

Kristal, Marc. "Hotel Health Clubs: The New Profit Centers." *Restaurant and Hotel Design*, July/August 1984, pp. 71-75.

Lachman, M. Leanne, and Martin, Dan. "Changing Demographics Shape Tomorrow's Real Estate Markets." *Urban Land*, November 1987, pp. 8-11.

Lawrence, Ron. "Club Location—Setting Your Sights on the Right Site." *IRSA Club Business*, April 1984, pp. 24-26.

Marcial, Gene G. "This New Fitness Club Has a New Wrinkle." *Business Week*, November 10, 1986, p. 112.

Masterson, Catherine. "Business as Usual: A Perilous Road?" *IRSA Club Business*, June 1987, pp. 35-40.

Maurstad, Tom. "Air Vita: Sweating Out Layovers in Style." *Advertising Age*, April 25, 1985, p. 38.

McCallum, Jack, and Keteyian, Armen. "Everyone's Doin' It." *Sports Illustrated*, December 3, 1984, pp. 72-86.

McCarthy, John. "What's the Best Hand for the Coming Year?" *IRSA Club Business*, October 1987, pp. 10-11.

———. "What's Up With the Y?" *IRSA Club Business*, June 1987, pp. 77-78.

Monroe, Linda. "Fitness Centers as Amenities." *Buildings*, July 1986, pp. 60-63.

Nash, Heyward L. "Instructor Certification—Making Fitness Programs Safer." *Parks and Recreation*, December 1986, pp. 24-30.

National Sporting Goods Association. "Sports Participation in 1985." 1985.

Nelton, Sharon. "The Over-50 Exerciser Finds a Couple of Allies." *Nation's Business*, June 1985, p. 54.

Pheng, Sova. "Inside Racquet Sports." *Sports Style*, September 16, 1985, p. 79.

Picard, Maureen. "Making Light of a Workout." *Restaurant and Hotel Design*, April 1986, p. 32.

Powills, Suzanne. "Fitness Centers: Profit Centers?" *Hospitals*, July 20, 1986, pp. 52-54.

Rademan, Myles. "Ski Town Prediction: Obstacles Ahead." *Planning*, February 1987, pp. 17-21.

Rawson, Bob. "Looking Into Locker Rooms." *IRSA Club Business*, July 1987, pp. 69-76.

Robinson, John P. "Where's the Fitness Room?" *American Demographics*, March 1987, pp. 34-56.

Robinson, John P., and Yergin, Marc L. "The Fitness Habit." *American Demographics*, August 1985, p. 40.

Roch, Michelle. "One, Two, Three Invest." *Canadian Banker*, April 1987, pp. 6-12.

Rothlein, Lewis. "Fitness—New Game at Racquet Clubs." *Long Island Business*, April 16, 1986, pp. 43-45.

Rottman, Meg. "Expert Sees Multisports as Future Fitness Trend." *Footwear News*, January 6, 1986, p. 20.

Seabury, Jennifer. "The Price of Staying Fit." *City Sports* (San Francisco Edition), February 1988, p. 47.

Schaeffer, Charles. "The Price You'll Pay to Sweat," *Changing Times*, August 1987, pp. 38-40.

Schmitt, Richard. "Fiscal Fitness: Efforts to Regulate Health Clubs Fail to End Abuses." *Wall Street Journal*, April 3, 1987, p. 33.

Simmons Market Research Bureau. "Study of Media and Markets." January, 1985.

Stern, Rosella. "Getting Away From It All." *Forbes*, October 27, 1986, p. 334.

Tarpey, John. "Home Exercise Gear: Another Industry Gets Fat on Fitness." *Business Week*, January 28, 1985, p. 118.

Tegmeyer, Diane. "Getting Physical at the Airport." *Working Women*, July 1985, pp. 51-53.

Thresher, Alison. "Girth of a Nation." *Nation's Business*, December 1986, pp. 50-52.

Tobin, Jeff. "Healthy Way to the Future." *IRSA Club Business*, June 1987, pp. 50-56.

Toufexis, Anastasia. "Body Styler of the Rich and Famous." *Time*, December 2, 1985, pp. 88-89.

———. "Watch the Bouncing Body." *Time*, June 30, 1986, p. 74.

————. "Shake a Leg, Mrs. Plushbottom; the Old Fat Farm Ain't What It Used to Be." *Time*, June 2, 1986, pp. 78-81.

Villarosa, Linda. "Working Out at Work." *Essence Magazine*, March 1987, pp. 106-107.

Wolff, Craig. "City Tennis: It Takes Either Money or Time." *New York Times*, July 10, 1987, p. B6.

Worthy, Ford S. "Ship Out and Shape Up." *Fortune*, April 2, 1984, pp. 135-137.

Zeitchick, Norman. "Who Plays Tennis, and Why." *Tennis*, May 1987, pp. 42-43.

————. "Babes in Exerciseland." *Life*, February 1987, p. 30.

————. "FTC Staff Takes It Easy on Health-Spa Operations." *Consumer Reports*, November 1985, p. 643.

————. "Health Clubs Run by 501(c)(3) Organizations, Not Unrelated Business." *Journal of Taxation*, April 1985, p. 243.

————. "How to Calculate the Amount of Liability Insurance You Need." *Club Industry*, April 1988, pp. 52-53.

————. "Joining a Health Spa? Exercise Caution." *Changing Times*, October 1985, p. 22.

————. "Loan Proposals: Packaging for Your Banker." *IRSA Club Business*, June 1987, pp. 45-46.

————. "1988 Guide to Health Clubs." *City Sports* (San Francisco Edition), February 1988, pp. 37-43.

————. "Numbers to Live By." *APFC Quarterly*, Summer 1986, pp. 48-50.

————. "On Sports—Wallyball." *The Wall Street Journal*, February 14, 1986, p. 19.

————. "Paring Off Pounds at a Live-in Clinic." *Changing Times*, February 1986, pp. 71-74.

————. "Playing It Safe in the Fitness Game." *Business Week*, September 10, 1984, pp. 146-150.

————. "Pushing the Pulse of a Generation." *Life*, February 1987, p. 28.

————. "Tennis: Can We Stop the Slide." *IRSA Club Business*, May 1987, pp. 83-85.